William H. Blackburn

Saint Patrick, and the Early Church of Ireland

William H. Blackburn

Saint Patrick, and the Early Church of Ireland

ISBN/EAN: 9783337325725

Printed in Europe, USA, Canada, Australia, Japan

Cover: Foto ©Lupo / pixelio.de

More available books at **www.hansebooks.com**

Saint Patrick,

AND

THE EARLY CHURCH OF IRELAND.

BY THE
Rev. WM. M. BLACKBURN, D.D.,
AUTHOR OF
"William Farel," "Aonio Paleario," "Ulrich Zwingli," Etc., Etc.

PHILADELPHIA:
PRESBYTERIAN BOARD OF PUBLICATION,
No. 821 CHESTNUT STREET.

CONTENTS.

PREFACE.

The Myth and the Man—Book of Armagh—Writings of Saint Patrick—Evidences of Authenticity—Other Ancient Authorities—Modern Writers...................................... 7

CHAPTER I.

HOME AND PARENTAGE.

Alcluyd—Good Blood—Potitus the Presbyter—Calpurnius the Deacon, and Decurio—Culdee Cells—Conchessa—First Missions in Scotland—Ninian, a specimen 21

CHAPTER II.

THE YOUNG CAPTIVE.

Patrick Baptized—Foolish Legends—The Lad not a Saint—Pirates—Patrick Sold in Ireland—Tends the Cattle—Rough Days—Remembers his Sins—Turns to God—His Religion 39

CHAPTER III.

THE ESCAPE.

Dreams—The Fugitive—On Shipboard—A Storm—A Desert—A Strange Spell—Home Again—Dreams of Ireland—Will be a Missionary 54

CHAPTER IV.

THE FAILURES OF PALLADIUS.

Early Missions in Ireland—Churches—Celestine Interested—Palladius Sent—Not well Received—Goes to Scotland—His Disciples—Servanus—Ternanus.................................. 63

CHAPTER V.

SIFTING THE LEGENDS.

Germanus—Stories of Patrick's Wanderings—Climax of Fable—Was Patrick ever at Rome?—Was he Sent forth by the Bishop of Rome?—Silence of Ancient Authors on the Question—Sechnall—Fiacc—Prosper—Bede—Patrick Confounded with Palladius—Silence of the Confession—Roman Mission a Legend.. 75

CHAPTER VI.

AMONG THE DATES.

When did Patrick go to Ireland to Preach?—Where Labour before he Went?—Any ties with Germanus?—Germanus and Lupus in Britain—Glastonbury—Movement in Armorica—Patrick Goes to Ireland—Young at Forty-five...... 96

CHAPTER VII.

FIRST LABOURS OF PATRICK IN IRELAND.

An Affrighted Herdsman—A Wrathy Master—Patrick not a Pirate—Fury Calmed—Preaching in a Barn—A Church Rises—Patrick's Visit to his Old Master—Repulse—Looking toward Tarah—The Young Benignus—Patrick's Tent before Tarah.. 110

CONTENTS.

CHAPTER VIII.

THE DRUIDS.

Cutting the Mistletoe—Sacrifices—Baal—Sun-worship—Druids' Doctrines—Priests—Superstitions—Holy Wells—Charms—Beltine Fires—Bards—Scotch Plaids—Irish Hospitality—Danger from the Druids.................................. 123

CHAPTER IX.

SAINT PATRICK'S ARMOUR.

Great Feast at Tarah—King sees Patrick's Fire—The Court on the Move—Patrick in the Great Hall Preaching—Dubtach and Fiacc Listen—The Hymn of Patrick................. 140

CHAPTER X.

CAUSES OF SUCCESS.

A Commanding Presence—Conall Converted—Mode of Teaching—King's Daughters—Doctrine of the Trinity—Legend of the Shamrock—Treatment of Superstition—The Crom-cruach—Patrick destroys the Great Idol—Pagan Customs Adopted by Christians—Centres of Influence—Love of Pioneering—Enthusiasm—Patrick's Extended Travels—Daring Spirit—Goes into Connaught—Robbed—Many Baptized—Endurances—Refusals of Gifts—Attention to Young Men—Redemption of Captives—All done in the Name of the Lord—Willing to be a Martyr—Power of Prayer—National Form of Early Christianity in Ireland—Persecution—Patrick's Charioteer dies in place of his Master—The Leinster Men.................................. 151

CHAPTER XI.

PATRICK'S CREED.

His Confession—Tillemont's View of it—The Doctrines in it—Occasion of the Epistle to Coroticus—Christian Captives—Noble Appeal by Patrick—An Embassy Scorned—Doctrines of the Epistle.......... 183

CHAPTER XII.

THE CHURCH OF SAINT PATRICK.

Theme of Controversy—Students under Patrick—Cell of Ciaran—Culdee System of Schools—Young Men ordained Bishops—Fiacc made Bishop of Sletty—Certain Conclusions—More Bishops than Churches—Her Synods—Glory of the Early Irish Church—The Decline—Invasions by Danes and English—Henry II. delivers Ireland to the Pope—Two Churches in Ireland—Strange Reversions in History.......... 196

CHAPTER XIII.

LAST DAYS.

Reform of the Laws—Patrick's Purgatory—Old Age—Toiling to the Last—St. Brigid—Patrick dies—Ireland in grief—"Litany of St. Patrick"—Canonization—True Character... 220

PREFACE.

THERE is profit in "guesses at truth," when they expose errors long and widely prevalent. They are like links of circumstantial evidence, no one of them singly of much positive value, but when joined and welded, they make a chain not easily broken. They are probabilities, and, according to their degree of strength, they afford convictions of certainty. I do not claim to set forth in this volume a series of events all of which are the undoubted verities of history. I do claim that the statements are as near to the complete truth concerning the subject treated as it has been possible for me to exhibit them after long and laborious research.

No concession is made to superstition by giving the title of "saint" to the man whose name has become so popular, and, after fourteen hundred years, is still as fresh as the shamrock and green as the emerald. Without the title he would hardly be identified or seen in his distinctive character. A good gospel word was abused when Rome assumed to confer upon eminent Christians the honour of being saints, and limited the term to them. By the New Testament charter we may claim it for all true Christians, however humble or unknown.

Was there ever such a man as Saint Patrick? It was wise to consider this question before attempting to write his life. By some it has been doubted, by a few others denied. But in such cases there has usually been a strong party feeling, or an ignorance of certain original sources of history. There is a distinction to be made between the myth and the man. Imagination has given us a Robinson Crusoe; the real man was Alexander Selkirk. The Saint Patrick of the ordinary Irish heart is certainly very mythical. The portrait of him was drawn from imagination; the colours are not those of the fifth, but those of the twelfth or fourteenth century. The deeds are manufactured to order and by the job, and the life is made of the baldest legends. This Patrick is a fully-developed Papist of the time, when certain errors prevailed, which he could not have known in the fifth century. He is constantly working miracles, some of them very trifling, and some of them astounding, beyond all that was ever recorded of a mere man. For his especial benefit divine revelations are made to him, which cause a greater amazement than any ever made to Moses or Paul. He is too wonderful to be real. The myth business was entirely overdone. The manufacturers did not perceive that common sense might some time be restored to the human race.

In the Middle Ages "it was customary with the monks to exercise their scholars in writing the lives of imaginary saints; asserting that it was a pious and very improving way of exercising the imagination!! The best of these fanciful biographies were laid aside for future use; and after the lapse of a few ages, when their statements could not be disproved, were produced and published as genuine.

It is said the monks of Holywell applied to De Stone, a writer of the thirteenth century, to write for them the life of their patron saint. He asked for materials, but on being informed that they had none, he volunteered to write it without any. In this way the lives of St. Patrick were greatly multiplied, and were filled with the most marvellous legends." *

Dr. Geoffrey Keating, more than two hundred years ago, said: "We are informed by a manuscript chronicle of antiquity that sixty-four persons have severally written the life of this reverend missionary." As to the " antiquity," it would not have been so very antique with most of them. Dr. Lanigan, a Roman Catholic historian, felt ashamed of the legend-makers, and he says of these lives that "they are full of fables, and seem to have been copied, either from each other, or from some common repository in which such stories have been collected. It would be idle to mention the many proofs which they exhibit of being patched up at a late period." And Bollandus, one of their learned writers, says concerning them, "They have been patched together by most fabulous authors, and are none of them more ancient than the twelfth century." This is not said of all the accounts given of Patrick by the annalists, some of whom wrote at a much earlier period. It is said of the fuller lives. In them is seen Patrick, the myth.

Very different was the man Patrick. If we strip away the burdening growth of wild ivies, we may get at the

* Ireland and the Irish, by Kirwan (Rev. N. Murray, D.D.) This title was given to a series of letters published in the N. Y. *Observer*, 1856, and to which I am much indebted.

genuine sturdy oak of his character. Even the grossest fables may have a foundation in fact. Often in the legends of the monks there can be traced a thread of historic truth. If we cast away the rubbish without sifting, we may lose a few gems hidden in the mass. If we allow that the so-called miracles of Patrick are most absurd, it does not at all follow that the history is a romance. Dr. Murray said: "Whilst there are many and good reasons for the rejection of the lives of Saint Patrick as so many monkish fables, as stupid as they are nonsensical, yet that there was a very devoted and greatly useful missionary of that name, endued with apostolical zeal, in Ireland, and about the time to which history refers, we are compelled to admit."

Traditions are of some value in regard to his existence and general history. "The traditions in the Book of Armagh," says Dr. Todd, "cannot be later than the third half century after the date usually assigned to the death of Saint Patrick. They assume his existence as admitted by all parties and never questioned. Had the story of Saint Patrick been then of recent origin, some remarks or legends in the collection would certainly have betrayed the fact. That the collectors of these traditions indulged in the unscrupulous use of legend strengthens the argument. There were men alive, at the time, whose grandfathers might have conversed with the disciples of the Patrick who was said to have converted the Irish in the latter half of the fifth century. Had the existence of this Patrick been a thing to be proved, or even doubted, some of these men would have been produced as witnesses, and made to tell their experience." For there was a great assumption made; it was that Armagh had a right to the jurisdiction over all other churches in Ireland—a claim not generally admitted. To prop it up these traditions were collected. All was based upon the existence and acts of Patrick, and yet in this curious record there is no attempt to *prove* that he had actually lived in Ireland. A whole people was ready to admit it—so ready indeed that, upon their admission and high regard for the man, is built up a very faulty theory of church authority. The foundation was solid—the structure was of wood, hay, stubble.

"It is incredible that a whole nation could have combined thus to deceive themselves; and it is even more incredible that a purely mythological personage should have left upon a whole nation so indelible an impression of imaginary services—an impression which continues to the present day in their fireside lore, their local traditions, the warm-hearted devotion and gratitude; which has left also its lasting memorial in the ancient names of hills and headlands, towns and villages, churches and monasteries throughout the country." *

Nor is this all. There are certain writings which claim to have come from the very pen of Saint Patrick. One is a hymn, which gives us no historic information, but is of great value in a spiritual light. It will be found in chapter ix., with the reasons for giving it a place in this volume. The only others which I assume to be genuine are the *Confessio Patricii*, and the *Epistola ad Coroticum*. Some writers include them both under either one of these titles, or refer to them as the "Cotton MS." It is only in their

* Todd. St. Patrick, preface.

simpler, and doubtless earliest form, that they are thus admitted; what is evidently interpolated by later hands is almost all rejected. They are quite universally admitted to be authentic and genuine by Protestant historians, some of whom also give a place to certain tracts, such as *De Tribus Habitaculis*. The evidence in favour of the Confession is somewhat stronger than that for the Epistle; but both are adopted, for the following reasons:

1. Their antiquity. They are older than any of the lives extant, and they are largely quoted in almost all the biographies. If one goes to a Romish book-stall, he may find, under their titles, a mixture of facts and ridiculous fables. But the older copies come to us with a more honest face and better credentials. About the close of the eighth century a copy of the Confession was transcribed into the collection entitled the Book of Armagh. The copyist complains that the original was becoming quite obscure, which is no slight evidence of authenticity. At the close are the words, "Thus far the volume which Patrick wrote with his own hand."

This copy is much shorter than those found in later manuscripts. Did the transcriber condense or abridge the copy before him? So thought Dean Graves, for an *et cetera* sometimes occurs. But this might only mean that the original was dim by reason of its age, or that only the leading facts of Patrick's life were intended to be preserved in the Armagh collection. It was not, however, the fashion of that age to abridge documents by leaving out the wonders and miracles; the style was rather to leave out the sober facts of history. If we find in this copy chiefly

PREFACE. 13

facts, we may conclude that the miracles were not yet invented. The Epistle to Coroticus is not in the Book of Armagh. But it bears the marks of the same age and authorship. It also quotes the Latin version of the Bible, made before that of Jerome, which Patrick would hardly have used, for the older translation would have won his heart in his younger days.

2. Their purity. They are not entirely free from errors; but the errors are just such as we should expect to find in the writings of a man in the decline of the fifth century. An orthodox Augustine was a rare being at a little earlier period. But the older copies of these writings are free from ridiculous legends of miracles and saint-worship. As such fables are contained only in later copies, we may infer that they were foisted in by the makers and mongers of huge fictions. Of the Confession, Neander says: "The work bears in its simple, rude style an impress that corresponds entirely to Patrick's stage of culture. There are to be found in it none of the traditions which, perhaps, proceeded only from English monks [after the Anglo-Saxon invasion in the twelfth century]; nothing wonderful, except what may be explained on psychological principles. All this vouches for the authenticity of the piece." * Neander knew the edition of Sir James Ware; that in the Book of Armagh is still purer. I have consulted the *Liber Ardmeachæ* in Sir William Bentham's *Irish Antiquarian Researches*.

3. Their design. It was not to prop up certain theories of church government. They were not written in the interest

* Hist. Ch. Church, ii. p. 122, *note*.

of any party, certainly not that of the Roman power. Such a purpose is manifest only in some of the later interpolations, thrust in when it was thought desirable to make the people believe that Ireland had received her great bishop and her Christianity directly from the banks of the Tiber. Dr. Todd says of the Confession, especially: "If it be a forgery, it is not easy to imagine with what purpose it could have been forged." * If a "pious fraud," it was by one who thought it important to assume the name and to set forth the experiences of Patrick in accordance with Scripture. Would such a man forge such a document?

The avowed object was to show why Patrick felt called to preach the gospel to the Irish people; to declare that he was not sent by man, but by the Lord; to furnish evidence that God had approved of his mission and labours; to record some of his experiences; to "make known God's grace and everlasting consolation, and to spread the knowledge of God's name in the earth." He wished in his old age "to leave it on record after his death, for his sons whom he had baptized in the Lord." In the proper places I have referred to this work as a defence of himself and his mission, and to the Epistle as a noble appeal for Christian rights and liberty.

4. *Their scriptural character.* Not the "fathers," but the inspired writers are quoted. "They abound in simple statements of Gospel truth; but there cannot be discovered in them a single one of those doctrines invented in later times, and set forth as necessary to salvation, in the Creed of Pope Pius IV. The Scriptures are treated by him with

* Saint Patrick, p. 347.

deep reverence, as infallible and sufficient. In support of his teaching, Patrick appeals to no other authority than to that of the written Word; and in the few chapters of his Confession alone there are thirty-five quotations from the Holy Scriptures." *

5. The honesty, humility and gratitude everywhere apparent. The Confession "is altogether such an account of himself as a missionary of that age, circumstanced as Saint Patrick was, might be expected to compose." Says Dr. Todd: "Its Latinity is rude and archaic." Its tone is: "I, Patrick, a sinner, a rustic, the least of all the faithful—" "a poor, sinful, despicable man—" not at all "on a level with the apostles—" "appointed a bishop in Ireland, I certainly confess that, by the grace of God, I am what I am."

Yet here an objection has been urged. "Who can believe," asks Casimir Oudin, "if Patrick was a man of learning and celebrity in the fifth century, that he could have written in a semi-Latin and barbarous style?" But it is not claimed that he was a man of learning, educated on the Continent, and passing thirty-five years in monasteries. Such a view is not consistent with what we know of the man. We should expect his pen to move in a rude style. The very objection is rather one of the strongest arguments for the authenticity of these writings. "The rude and barbarous Latinity" does not appear in the tracts concerning the "Three Habitations" and the "Twelve Abuses of the Age;" one of which has been attributed to

* Church of St. Patrick, by the Rev. John Wilson, Belfast, 1860. This is a valuable tract.

Augustine of Hippo, and the other to Cyprian. The writer's own account is that he could not write elegantly, for he had not been a student from infancy, and he had been so long among a rude people that his speech had been changed to another tongue. In our times well-educated missionaries in foreign lands, grown familiar with a foreign tongue, can appreciate his difficulty. He did not write as a monk, but as a missionary.

6. The neglect into which the older form of these writings fell is some evidence of their truth. They did not serve the purposes of a Church which has coolly laid claim to all the saintly characters from the time of Abel to the beginning of the fifteenth century. She has swelled the catalogue of saints, but she has never been content with the original records of good men. She has added to them whatever suited her purpose, and cast into the shade the original documents. Thus has she done with the Holy Scriptures. How much has she added to the first simple accounts of Mary and Peter, and even our Lord! Her very neglect of the original records is an argument for their authenticity. It sets them apart from the legends which were manufactured in her interest. It distinguishes the true coin from the cheap counterfeit, the latter having become very profitable to Rome. Her authors have not been content to publish these unvarnished writings of an honest Christian missionary. There was not enough of the wonderful, the monkish, the Romish element in them. They were cast into a dark corner, according to her manner of putting to silence the witnesses of truth. The real Patrick has been slumbering his thousand years. It is

time for him to rouse, and in rising up he will throw off the vast heaps of superstitions piled upon him to keep him quiet.

Here, then, is a footing upon these ancient documents. Assuming their genuineness, we may be guided to some knowledge of the life, the labours and doctrines of Patrick. What agrees with them we shall accept from all sources within reach; what is inconsistent is rejected.

Among the oldest of the "Lives" is the brief *Hymn of Fiacc*, or St. Fiech, who seems to have been a disciple of Patrick. If he composed such a poem, he may have sung it as a converted bard; but a later hand is apparent in a few miracles added to it. I have before me a tri-form copy, containing the original Irish, the Latin version of Colgan, and an English translation by the anonymous author of a Life of St. Patrick.* The collection of "Lives" in *Colgan's Trias Thaumaturga* is valuable, if defects in quality can be made good by superabundance in quantity, the *Tripartite Life* being the only one worthy of much regard. The reading of *Joceline's Life of St. Patrick* almost disgusted me with the subject, but it was refreshing to find one of the latest Romish writers saying, "How derogatory from common sense have the biographers of our saint acted, and particularly Joceline!" Our modern author, however, is not clear of the same fault.

Almost all my previous researches might have been spared had I received at an earlier day the work entitled *St. Patrick, Apostle of Ireland; a Memoir of his Life and Mission, with an introductory dissertation on some early*

* Baltimore: John Murphy, 1861.

usages of the Church in Ireland . . . by James Henthorn Todd, D.D. To this learned work by an Episcopal clergyman, and "an antiquarian declared to be thoroughly versed in Irish history," my indebtedness is gratefully acknowledged. His brother, the Rev. Wm. G. Todd, in his *Church of St. Patrick*, has proved that the ancient Church of Ireland was independent of Rome.

Other works have been consulted, such as the Historia Britonum of Nennius; Ecclesiasticæ Historiæ Gentes Anglorum, of Bede; Britannicarum Ecclesiarum Antiquitates, of Ussher; Annales Ecclesiastici of Baronius; Mémoires Ecclesiastique, par M. de Tillemont; Le Grand Dictionnaire, par M. Louis Moreri; Biographie Universelle; Annales Hiberniæ, ab Thoma Carve; Collectanea de Rebus Hibernicis, by Charles Vallancy; Les Moines d'Occident, par le Comte de Montalembert; Alban Butler's Lives of the Saints; Ledwich's Antiquities of Ireland; Annals of Ireland, by the Four Masters; Neander's Memorials of Christian Life; Ecclesiastical Histories of Ireland, by Brenan, Carew, Lanigan and Wordsworth; Sir James Ware's History and Antiquities of Ireland; McLauchlan's Early Scottish Church; Soames' Latin Church during Anglo-Saxon Times; Lappenberg's History of England under the Anglo-Saxon Kings; the several Histories of Ireland by Keating, Macgeoghan, Moore, Haverty, O'Halloran and O'Connor; and the General Histories of the Christian Church by Fleury, Neander, Mosheim, Kurtz, Cave and Collier.

I have not discussed at tedious length the question of Saint Patrick's birth-place, but have frequently pointed out evidences that it was on the Clyde. The opinion that it

PREFACE. 19

was Boulogne-sur-Mer, in Gaul, seems to be quite modern. Its chief supporter is Dr. Lanigan, who ingeniously brings forward no little learning on the subject, but all his trimming of antiquated names can hardly satisfy us that his Bononia Tarvannæ was Patrick's Bonavem Taberniæ, where the great missionary tells us his father dwelt. We can find half a dozen places in Gaul once called Bononia,* and a score of Taberniæ; and possibly by Dr. Lanigan's mode of reasoning we might show that Saint Patrick was born at the Three Taverns (*Tres Tabernas*), where Paul met his Christian brethren. This would bring the "Apostle of Ireland" near enough to Rome, in his childhood, to please the most ardent papal admirers. The opinion that he was born on the banks of the Clyde, or somewhere in North Britain, is supported by Fiacc and his scholiast, the author of St. Declan's Life, Probus, Sigibert (quoted by Ussher), Cave, Ware, Joceline, Fleury, Tillemont, Bailet, Alban Butler, Macgeoghan, Baronius (?), Moreri, Spottiswoode, Camden, Collier, Lappenberg, Thorpe, Henry, Gibbon, Neander, Milner, Wordsworth, J. C. Robertson, Hetherington, D'Aubigné, McLauchlan, Giesseler, Kurtz, Mosheim, Todd, Reeves and other writers, both Protestant and Roman Catholic.

Truth and fact have been most earnestly sought, and the attempt is to present them intelligibly and impartially. I have given to many statements the heavy shading of a doubt, and I only ask for them the benefit of a probability. A plain mark has been put upon every silly legend, which it seemed proper to notice in order to make clear the points

* Anthon's Class. Dict.

of the case, or to bring upon some popular superstition its deserved ridicule.

If the name of Saint Patrick were less known; if it had fallen into obscurity; if we had to rescue it from oblivion, as that of Hyppolitus or that of Paleario has been rescued, and if he were not so commonly portrayed in colours that do not at all suit his complexion,—ours would be an easier task. It would be less difficult to meet the popular views. In telling the truth about him we must come in conflict with the common opinions. Men will take down their histories and cyclopedias and read the usual story, shake their heads, call in question what we relate, and examine the subject no further; I can only ask them to follow up my references.

If any one attached to the Roman Catholic Church shall read this volume, let him not suppose that we dishonour the great man whom he reveres as the patron saint of all Irishmen. Far from it; we would have him honored in his true character. If such a reader will adopt the ancient religion of Saint Patrick, he will find himself almost a modern Protestant. At all events, he will go to the Word of God as the only authority in matters of faith, and the only source of light to guide him in the way of life. It is not so much our aim to set forth the man Patrick as it is to illustrate the principles by which he was controlled in the labours that have made his name renowned. The record of his toils and triumphs ought to be instructive, if a late writer says truly, "From all that can be learned of him, there never was a nobler Christian missionary than Patrick."

CHICAGO, ILL. W. M. B.

SAINT PATRICK.

CHAPTER I.

HOME AND PARENTAGE.

IN cottages, near little towns, great men have been born. God makes his earnest workers of dust, that he may have all the glory. When looking for the birth-place of Saint Patrick we turn to Scotland. The voyager on the deck of the vessel that steams up the Clyde will have his eye upon a lonely, rugged rock that rises almost three hundred feet above the water, and is now crowned with a castle. It was once called Alcluyd,* the Rock of the Clyde. It gave its name to a fort on its top and a town at its foot. There, on their own frontier, the ancient Britons resisted the Northern Scots and Picts. Border strifes made it a place of death. The old songs tell of the rivers running red with blood. It

* Alcluith, Alcluaid, Alcluada, Alclyde. In Ossian's poems it is Balclutha. See my preface.

seems to have been a stronghold of the Romans, who built one of their walls from Alcluyd across the country to the Frith of Forth. To them the Britons yielded and looked for defence during several generations. It is supposed that these Romanized Britons united with the tribes of Southern Scotland and formed the Cumbrian league, or the kingdom of Strathclyde. Their capital was Alcluyd, which they named Dunbriton, "the hill of the Britons," whence the present name of Dumbarton. Four miles from it, toward Glasgow, on the line of the old Roman wall, is the modern town of Kilpatrick, which claims to be the birth-place of Saint Patrick. The Christian year 397 is the most probáble date of his birth.

The account given in his name is this: "I, Patrick, a sinner, the rudest and the least of all the faithful, and the most despicable among most people, had for my father Calpurnius, a deacon, son of the late Potitus, a presbyter, who was of the town of Bonavem Taberniæ; for he had a cottage (or farm) in the neighbourhood where I was captured."*

---

* Confessio Patricii. We have stated in the preface the reasons for presuming the Confession, in its oldest form, to be genuine.

He does not tell us where he was born; he simply relates that his father dwelt at Bonavem, where he also was living when taken captive. But why mention the place as his home, unless he was a native of it? The plain inference is that he was born there. It is difficult to identify Bonavem Taberniæ with any ancient town. To no one probably was this Latin name given; it is simply the Latin translation of some name which was foreign to the language of the Romans. Perhaps the words mean a town at the *river's mouth*,* near the *tents* (taberniæ) or shops of the Roman army. The Hymn of Fiacc begins thus: "Patrick was born at Nempthur." The old commentator upon it says of Nempthur, "It is a city in North Britain, viz. Alcluada." According to the ancient and best traditions, we may assume that Saint Patrick was born in a cottage not far from Alcluyd, and under its protection.

But, feeling that he was unworthy of any birthplace, he did not clearly define it. In his old age he thought rather of his home in the heavens. He might have said, as did Severinus, one of the first

---

* *Bon*, mouth; *aven*, river.—*Celtic Dict.* Nempthur may come from *Nem*, a river, and *Tur*, a tower—the castle on the river.

missionaries along the banks of the Danube, in the fifth century: "What pleasure can it be to a servant of God to specify his home, or his descent, since by silence he can so much better avoid all boasting? I would that the left hand knew nothing of the good works which Christ grants the right hand to accomplish, in order that I may be a citizen of the heavenly country. Why need you know my earthly country, if you know that I am truly longing after the heavenly? But know this, that God has commissioned me to live among this heavily oppressed people."

The admiring monks sought to glorify Saint Patrick by inventing for him a royal lineage. They ran it back to Britus, or Britanus, the supposed ancestor of the Britons. But he had no such vain imaginations. It was enough for him to tell us of his grandfather. We are glad to know that he was the grandson of Potitus,* the presbyter. The blood was good. If he had thought that his grandfather had disgraced himself by marriage,† he

---

* "Son of Odisse" is added on the margin of the Book of Armagh, in the hand of the original scribe. In Fiacc's Hymn he is called "the Deacon Odisse."

† In the year 314, the council of Neocæsarea decreed that the presbyter who married should forfeit his standing.

would hardly have mentioned him as a minister of God's word. He would have been silent about his clerical ancester. It seems that he did not believe in the celibacy of the clergy, even in his old age. Here is some proof of the truth and the antiquity of "the Confession." If it had been invented and written in more papal times, Saint Patrick would not have been made the grandson of a presbyter; not if that presbyter held the rank of a Roman priest.* The book must be older than the notion that the early Churches of Scotland and Ireland were controlled by the bishop of Rome.

Of Potitus we learn nothing more, except that his office was held in high esteem in his times. Martin of Tours declared, at a public entertainment, that the emperor was inferior in dignity to a presbyter.† This may have been a boast, yet without vaunting the early Christians of Scotland

Stronger ground was gradually taken, until, about the year 400, the bishop of Rome forbade the marriage of the clergy. But yet, in remoter regions, his bull was not closely heeded.— *Neander's Ch. Hist.* ii. 147.

* Some writers call Potitus a *priest.* Thus Innes, Brenan, Carew and other Romanists. The original word is rendered *presbyter* by such prelatists as Todd, Soames and Ussher.

† Mosheim, Cent. V. chap. ii.

regarded the presbyter as a bishop. The same was true in England and Ireland. Even in the tenth century, Elfric, a Saxon bishop, wrote thus of the orders of church officers, putting the presbyter first: "There is no difference between him and the bishop, except that the bishop is appointed to confer ordination, which, if every presbyter should do, would be committed to too many. Both, indeed, are one and the same order." Pryne says of the early Britons: "They maintain the parity of the bishops and presbyters." In Eastern lands men began to put a difference between these officers. "Yet a Chrysostom and a Jerome still asserted the primitive equal dignity of the presbyters and the bishops, very justly believing that they found authority for this in the New Testament."*

Potitus may have been a Culdee presbyter. His Latin name does not prove that he was a Roman, sent out with the army from Rome as a missionary to the Britons. Native names were often Latinized by the historians.† It is more likely that he was a Briton by birth. Perhaps he studied

---

* Neander's Ch. Hist. vol. ii. p. 155, American ed.

† Succath was changed to Patricius. Two native ministers in the sixth century, near Loch Ness, are called Emchadus and Virolecus.

the Scriptures and prayed in the Culdee cell at Alcluyd, and at its door preached to the people.

To us there is something quite romantic about the *cuil, kil,* or cell of the early Christians in Scotland and Ireland. There is scarcely a doubt that it gave name to the *Cuildich,* or Culdees. To them there was a sacredness about it as they retreated to it in some lonely wood, narrow valley, or rugged ravine. It was not the abode of a monk; it was the resort of a missionary. It was his "study," where he prepared for preaching. Its origin we cannot discover; perhaps it was, at first, a refuge from enemies or a resort for prayer. It became the sacred place of the presence of God; almost the Holy of Holies, with its veil rent for the entrance of the Culdee worshipper. Its plan was carried with every missionary, and he chose the spot for his "cell" as the Hebrew did for the tabernacle. There was his sanctuary; there he wrestled with God in prayer; there the people might assemble with reverence to hear him preach. It was holy ground; the burning bush was there in the desert. The cell develops into three forms— the oratory, the kirk and the college.* At some

* Princeton Review, 1867. Article on "The Culdee Monasteries."

period a cell, or kil, was located near the spot where Saint Patrick was born. It may have been close by the same cottage. There Potitus may have studied and prayed. There the people may have assembled for worship. There, it seems, a Culdee kirk, or church, grew up, which the people of later days called Kilpatrick, in honour of the great missionary, who was born at the place. Potitus seems to have lived to a good old age, and been worthy of the respect of his grandson. It is some proof of his excellent family government that he reared a deacon.

The deacon was Calpurnius. What sort of a deacon was he? Some place him in "the third or lowest order of the ordained clergy." Such "deacon's orders" would savour of Rome, and give to Calpurnius the rank of a clergyman. If he was such a deacon, he was quite free from the Roman notions of celibacy, for he took a wife and reared a family. If a clergyman at all, he must have been a Culdee licentiate. It was held to be no sin for a Culdee minister to marry. But if he was a Culdee deacon, he was hardly a minister, or a candidate for the ministry. The church of the Culdees seems to have been regulated after the Bible, and not after the Roman model. It appears to have had deacons, elders and presbyters, and none of higher rank. Doubtless the early Culdees had no very perfect system of church government, but in what they did have, they sought to follow "the order of the primitive Church." Dwelling among quarrelsome tribes, and in danger of persecutions, they gave themselves to preaching Christ and peace, rather than to questions and modes of government.* Calpurnius may have been a deacon of the church at Alcluyd.

Another office is said to have been held by Calpurnius. If a certain ancient letter came from the hand of Saint Patrick, he says, "I was of a family respectable according to the flesh, my father having been a decurio. I gave up my nobility for the good of others, that I might be a missionary."† The decurio was a magistrate and counsellor in the Roman colonies. The office conferred a high rank on those who held it. These officers "were members of the court, or counsellors of the city, and could not be ordained [to the Christian ministry]. By virtue of their estates they were tied to the offices of their country. They must have a certain

* Hetherington's Hist. Church of Scotland. Chapter i.
† The Epistle concerning Coroticus. See my preface.

amount of property."* Such was the law of Constantine for the more wealthy decuriones. "The fact that Calpurnius is said to have held that office may perhaps tend to show us that he belonged to one of the Roman provinces of Great Britain, rather than to Bretagne Armorique. It is a mistake to suppose that a decurio was necessarily a military officer."† Such a man must have had no little authority over the Britons of Strathclyde. The Romans allowed "governors of the native races," especially at Alcluyd. When the Romans were called home to resist the Goths, they must have left very much of their power in the hands of the magistrate. But Calpurnius ruled in the State like a good deacon of the Church.

Tradition informs us that the mother of Saint Patrick was Conchessa. Various writers call her the sister of Martin, archbishop of Tours and the founder of monasteries in Western Europe. A candid Romanist thinks that this opinion is refuted by the silence of the ancient annalists. "For it cannot be supposed that a connection so honourable, and which, if it existed, must have been generally known, could have been passed over in

---

* Bingham's Ecclesiastical Antiquities, book iv. 4.
† Todd's Saint Patrick. Dublin, 1864, p. 354.

silence by persons who must have been eager to mention whatever could exalt the character of Saint Patrick with posterity."* In the tract on "the mothers of the saints in Ireland,"† she is represented as a Briton. We may believe that she was "a woman superior to the majority of her sex," and that she endeavoured to instil into the heart of her son the doctrines of Christianity.‡

Such a family, in which there was a presbyter and a deacon, dwelling on the banks of the Clyde, could not well be the solitary Christians of that country. There must have been many others. Whence their religion, and how long had it existed in Scotland?

Missionaries may have followed in the footsteps of the Roman army, the sword preparing the way for the cross. For four hundred years after Christ the Romans held sway over many parts of England and Southern Scotland, and the door was open for teachers of the faith, however severely some of the emperors persecuted them. Yet little seems to have been done. The native people hated the

* An Ecclesiastical History of Ireland, by the Right Rev. P. J. Carew, p. 52.
† Attributed to Ængus the Culdee, of the ninth century.
‡ D'Aubigné's Hist. of Ref. Vol. v. chap. i.

invaders; they were not likely to give ear to preachers who came from the Roman Empire. Missionaries from Rome would have taught certain Roman errors, such as the celibacy of the clergy, prelacy and submission to the bishop of Rome. We must not forget that Rome, in the first Christian centuries, was far purer than she became after the seventh; the great errors had not grown up: still, she had perverted many doctrines and practices before the Roman army left Britain. If we found these peculiar errors among the Christian Britons and Scots at an early day, we should conclude that they had been taught by Roman missionaries. We do not find them; we find a much purer form of Christianity; and our conclusion is, that they first received the gospel from a different quarter.

Ships sailed to Britain from Eastern lands where the Greek language prevailed. They came from the harbours of cities where the apostles had preached. On their decks may have been Christian merchants and missionaries from Greece and Asia Minor. The one class could supply funds, the other could give the gospel to the Scots and Britons. We may suppose that such teachers of the faith gathered a few people about them and told them of Jesus who was crucified for them. All wondered; some believed. The number of hearers increased. Little bands celebrated the dying love of Christ. The Druids shook their heads in anger; the people were forsaking them; their craft was in danger; they cried out against the new doctrines. They claimed to be the only religious teachers and the law-makers. They muttered their dark suspicions to the chieftains and kings. Persecution arose. The little flocks were scattered. They sought refuge in narrower valleys. The teachers hid in closer retreats. They made them cells for prayer and study, and became Culdees. In some such manner, we may suppose, Christianity was first planted in Scotland and the northern part of Britain, and the Culdees arose.* Before the end of the second century there appear to have been many bands of Christians north of the Clyde and the Roman Wall. In the year 234, Origen wrote in Greek, "The power of God, our Saviour, is even with them who in Britain are shut out from

* Another opinion is, that Southern Britain first received the missionaries from Asia Minor and Greece, or from the churches of Lyons and Marseilles, which were of the Grecian type; and that under such persecutions as that of Diocletian many of these early British Christians fled to Scotland and Ireland, where they took refuge in cells and became known as the Culdees.—*Buchanan, Rerum Scot. Hist.*

our world." About the same time Tertullian said "that parts of the British Isles, not reached by the Romans, were made subjects to Christ." This was scarcely all rhetoric. We know that early in the fifth century Rome sent "bishops" to the "Scots believing in Christ." She did it as if it were a new thing; without her aid the Scots had believed. They continued to believe and increase. They rejected her "bishops" until forced to accept them in the twelfth century. In their churches was a purer faith. "These churches were formed after the Eastern type; the Britons [and Scots] would have refused to receive the type of that Rome whose yoke they detested."*

We find in Ninian a specimen of an early Briton Christian. Perhaps he was known to Potitus; they were of the same kingdom of Strathclyde. He was born about the year 360. His parents were Christians and early devoted him to the Christian ministry. He loved his associates, abstained from jests, gave his hours to study and closely searched the Holy Scriptures. He was sparing of words, courteous in manners, moderate at the table and reserved in public. The body was ruled by the spirit that dwelt in it. He was marked

* D'Aubigné.

as a young man of warm zeal, deep humility and dauntless courage. Having passed through the schools of his own country, and still eager for knowledge, he went to Rome.

Ailred tells us that when Ninian came to Rome, the blessed youth wept over the relics of the apostles and gave himself to their care. If he did, he had no suspicion that a gross deception was practiced upon him. The " pope" received him as a son. He was thereupon handed over to certain teachers, who well knew how to manage a simple-hearted student. He soon discovered that his own people did not understand the Scriptures as men interpreted them at Rome. He was led to think that the Briton Christians were greatly in error, but on what points we are not informed. Doubtless they had simpler forms of worship; they had less regard for relics, outward rites, the sign of the cross, clerical rules and tonsure, festival days, liturgies and higher orders of clergy; they did not regard the bishop of Rome as the successor of St. Peter, nor as the bond of unity in the Christian Church. They held Christ as their master and the only King in Zion. The eyes of Ninian were blinded. He thought that his countrymen had not fully come up to the faith; he did not see that

Rome had begun to depart from it. He resolved to impart his new ideas to his brethren. The story is that the Roman bishop ordained him as "the first apostle" to his people, and sent him forth with his benediction.

When Ninian returned to his own country, he was received with great demonstrations of joy. The people gathered about him. They held him as one of the prophets. They praised Christ for what they saw and heard. They were not heathen, and yet "the *first* apostle to his own people" had come! Rome ignored the former teachers and presbyters: she now sent a "bishop." But they looked upon him as a follower of Christ and of his fathers. It is related that on his homeward way he had visited Martin of Tours, studied architecture, and brought with him a company of builders. A spot was chosen in the southern part of Galloway, near a deserted Roman camp, and the rallying-point of a Caledonian tribe. It was not far from the seat of a Culdee establishment. There a church was built of bright white stone; hence its name, *Candida Casa,* or Whitherne.*

---

* Now Whithorn. The town of this name is on the main shore. Near it is an island, which "has some remains of a very ancient small church, believed to have been one of the earliest

"There," says his biographer, "the candle being placed in its candlestick, it began to give forth its light, with heavenly signs to those who were in the house of God, and its graces radiating, those who were dark in their mind were enlightened by the bright and burning word of God, and the frigid were warmed." We reject the miracles ascribed to him by Ailred, who says they are "credible only by such as believe that nothing is impossible to the faithful." He seems to have laid aside his Roman notions, and assumed no high prelatic powers. He was doubtless an earnest missionary, labouring more to make converts to Christ than to Rome. In the wilds of Galloway he taught sound doctrine and scriptural discipline. "He opened his mouth with the word of God, through the grace of the Holy Spirit," says Ailred. "The faith is received, error is put away, the [heathen] temples are destroyed, churches are erected: men rush to the fountain of saving cleansing—the rich and the poor alike, young men and maidens, old men and children, mothers with their infants; renouncing Satan and all his works and pomps, they are joined to the family of believers by faith, and

stone structures of its class in Scotland."—*Nelson's Handbook to Scotland.*

word, and sacraments." Such was his work among the Southern Picts. Perhaps he extended his labours north of the Roman Wall. Who knows but that he visited Alcluyd, lodged with Calpurnius, filled the lad Patrick with wonder, and talked late into the night with the venerable Potitus? Who knows but that this aged presbyter convinced him of Rome's advance in error, and confirmed him in the ancient faith of the Culdees?

He seems to have done little for Rome and much for Christ. At a ripe age he died in peace. More than a score of Scottish churches were named in honour of this zealous missionary. Rome canonized him; it had been better if she had returned to his doctrines. That he was free from error we do not assert. We have endeavoured to sketch the man,* that we might have before us the portrait of a Christian Briton, who lived in the time of Saint Patrick's youth. No great missionary was more likely to influence the mind of the grandson of Potitus.

* Consult Bede's Eccl. Hist., McLauchlan's Early Scottish Church, The Spottiswoode Miscellany, Neander's Church History.

CHAPTER II.

THE YOUNG CAPTIVE.

WE may imagine the deacon Calpurnius walking solemnly by the side of the pale Conchessa, bearing an infant son in his arms, and turning to a fountain* near to a Culdee cell; then joining fervently in the simple services of worship, and praying silently that the Lord will bless his neighbours who gaze upon the scene; then listening to what is said of God's holy covenant with his people and their little ones, and holding forth his child to receive the token of its surrender to the Father, the seal of its redemption by the Son and the symbol of its renewal by the Holy Ghost. We almost see the reverent presbyter take his grandson and with the words of Christ apply to him the waters of baptism, give him the kiss of peace,† place him in the arms of the tearful

---

* Fountains and wells seem to have been used at an early period for baptism; they were afterward held sacred in Scotland and Ireland.

† An ancient custom.—*Thackeray's Ancient Britain*, vol. i. 198.

Conchessa, and lift his hands for the prayer and benediction. We are told that to this child was given the name of Succath in his baptism. At a later day he was called Patrick.*

In this we have supposed nothing more than may have been true. But the story-tellers of the Middle Ages imagined things that are hugely false, and made sad work of the life of Saint Patrick. Among their lying legends the facts are almost lost. Not content with marvels, they invented miracles. What wonders the child performed, even before he breathed! He is but an infant when he makes the sign of the cross on the ground, and on the spot a fountain flows whose waters cure the blind. Is the water flooding his mother's floor? He drops fire from his fingers and every drop is dried away. Does his aunt want a bundle of fagots? The boy Patrick brings ice in his arms and makes a rousing fire with it. Does his sister Lupita fall and bruise her forehead? He heals the wounds in an instant. While herding the flock

---

* Keating's Hist. of Ireland. Fiacc's Hymn runs: "Succat his name at the beginning." Succat in old British means "the god of war," or "strong in war." An odd name, says Lanigan, for the child of a Christian deacon. Not more odd than for Palladius to bear a name derived from the heathen goddess Pallas.—*Todd's St. Patrick*, 363.

he grows careless; a wolf comes and steals one of the finest lambs. The lad is reproved, but he prays all night, and lo! in the morning the roguish thief brings back the lamb, lays it unhurt at his feet, and then flees to the woods! Thus we might go on heaping up the nonsense found in the first thirteen chapters of a book written by Joceline, a monk of the twelfth century. No wonder that one Romish author rejects such legends as stories "foisted in by the credulous writers of those dark ages, who were for heaping miracles upon the backs of their saints which the present times are not expected to give credit to;" and another declares that they are "enough to rouse the indignation of every pious reader." It is high time for the Romanists to purge the old "Lives of the Saints" as thoroughly as the young Patrick is said to have cleaned the fortress and stables of the cruel lord of Dunbriton; for the story is, that the tyrant ordered Patrick's aunt to do the slavish job, but the lad came forward like a man, and by miracle made such a riddance of all trash that none was ever found afterward in the whole establishment.

We must believe that the young Patrick had all the human nature of a boy. He was not a saint. His deeds were not holy. It is far more likely that he complained of his oatmeal porridge at breakfast, and ran away from his mother to the trout-streams to catch something better for dinner; that when sent into town on an errand he took the "Rock on the Clyde" in his way, and loitered for an hour on the top looking for savage Highlanders; that he threw snowballs at some wandering Druid, or talked long with the Roman soldiers when he ought to have been tending his father's sheep.

He was taught the holy commandments,* but he did not keep them. He was "warned for his salvation," but he heeded not the preachers. "I knew not the true God," he said in his old age, as he looked back upon the days of his youth. He must have meant that he knew not God as his heavenly Father, nor Christ as his Saviour; he did not love him nor obey the truth. No doubt his parents taught him the way to be saved, for he seems to have remembered the lessons of home in his captivity. His grandfather must have had a Bible, and taught Patrick to read it, as Ninian was taught. But he had no heart for the truth. "He was fond of pleasure, and delighted to be the leader of his youthful companions. In the midst

* Confessio Patricii, near the beginning.

of his frivolities he committed a serious fault." *
What it was we know not; it proves that he was
not holy from his infancy—not "always a Christian," as Alban Butler declares him to have been. †
He was then fifteen years of age.

It was not always safe for him to lead a troop of
young friends down the Clyde to hold their sports
on its banks, or to stroll up the glen and make
merry with some jovial shepherd and his flock.
For pirates often drew their boats into some cove,
wandered over the hills, seized upon the playful
children, carried them away to strange lands and
sold them into slavery. With bolder steps they sometimes marched into villages, slew the strong men,
abused the aged, plundered the houses or set them
on fire, laid waste the gardens, stole the cattle and
took off the children. As Sir Walter Scott says of
the Danish pirates: "They were heathens, and did
not believe in the Bible, but thought of nothing
but battle and slaughter and making plunder."
Most of the Roman soldiers had been called home;
so few were left that they were not able to protect
the people along the Clyde.

One day a band of these robbers came like

---

* D'Aubigné.
† Lives of the Saints, March 17.

vultures upon the town, and, after every sort of outrage, they carried off Patrick and about two hundred of the villagers. The captives were placed in the boats,* and the prows were turned down the Clyde and toward Ireland. What sad thoughts in the mind of Patrick as he gazed back at the high rock so near his home! What anger toward the pirates! But he afterward saw a reason for it all; the hand of God was laid severely upon him to correct his evil ways. "I was taken captive, when I was nearly sixteen years old. I knew not the true God, and I was carried in captivity to Ireland, with many thousands† of men, according to our deserts, because we had gone back from God, and had not kept his commandments, and were not obedient to our priests, who used to warn us for our salvation. And the Lord brought upon us the wrath of his displeasure, and scattered us

---

*Curachs, no doubt made of wicker and covered with ox-hides. They were used by the people of the British Isles long after the Norwegians showed them how to build small ships.

† Not "many thousands" in his company, but "many thousands" in a like condition of bondage, taken away at various times and to various countries. We read of British captives at Rome in the sixth century, of whom Gregory said, "Non Angli, sed angeli."

among many nations, even unto the ends of the earth."*

Who were those pirates? Were they Irishmen, led by Niall of the Nine Hostages? This daring corsair roved over the seas, and excelled in the slave-trade before, we suppose, Saint Patrick was born. Those who fix his birth before the year 387 attribute the capture to Niall,† the ancestor of the O'Neills, and "martial hero of the Irish." Of him an ancient poet sings, that he,

> By force of arms, and martial skill,
> Subdued the rebels who opposed his right;
> And, as a pledge of their allegiance,
> Detained five hostages of noble blood;
> And, to secure the homage of the Scots,
> He kept confined four hostages of note;
> From whence this prince the ancient records call
> The Hero of the Nine Hostages.

On one of his excursions for plunder he was shot with an arrow and died on the spot. He was certainly great enough to carry away Saint Patrick, whose supposed miraculous power was strangely wanting at the time. But he appears not to have lived long enough for such a deed. It is more

---

* Conf. Pat.
† Keating, Lanigan, D'Aubigné, Wilson.

likely that the captors were led by some other chieftain. When the Romans were leaving the Clyde, the poor Britons were at the mercy of their foes. The old wall was no defence. On neither side of the line did the gospel of peace reign. The Picts shouted, the Britons groaned, and the Irish ran in and took the spoils and the prey.

There is another version of the story which merits a respectful notice. It is, that the capture was made in Brittany, in the North of France. Some writers, who think that Saint Patrick was not born near Boulogne, suppose that his parents left the Clyde and settled on the coast of Gaul.* The commentator on Fiacc's Hymn gives the legend thus: "This was the cause of the servitude of Patrick. His father, mother, brother and five sisters all went from the Britons of Alcluaid, across the Iccian sea southward, on a journey to the Britons of Letha. . . . Then came seven sons of Sectmaide, king of Britain, in ships. . . . and they made great plunder on the Britons of Armoric Letha, where Patrick with his family was, and they wounded Calpurnius there, and carried off Patrick and Lupait [his sister] with them to Ireland, and sold them."

* So D'Aubigné.

This story is usually supported by the fact that a colony of Northern Britons had lately settled in Gaul, giving to that region the name of Brittany, if indeed the Brittani had not dwelt there centuries before. It was at first a Roman military colony, consisting of British warriors. "Though that country had from the earliest times, by descent, language and Druidism, been related to Britain, yet the new colonists, who were followed by many others, both male and female, served unquestionably to bind more closely and to preserve the connection between Bretagne and the Britons of Wales and Cornwall. . . . But Britain was thereby deprived of her bravest warriors, and thence the more easily became an early prey to foreign invaders. Scots, Picts and Saxons continued to trouble it."* This colony might have resisted the pirates more strongly than the dwellers on the Clyde. If Patrick had been there, he might have been safe; if his parents were fleeing thither for safety, he may have been captured on the way. But the whole story seems to be founded in the wish to connect Saint Patrick with the Romans and the Roman

* Lappenberg's Hist. of England under the Anglo-Saxon Kings, vol. i. pp. 7, 59; Thackeray's Ancient Britain, vol. ii. p. 72.

Church. The better authorities do not support it. The second, third and fourth "Lives" in Colgan's collection make Patrick to have been captured "near Alcluaid," by a fleet of Irish pirates. About six years later he is found at home again with his parents in Britain, a country named as one entirely distinct from Gaul.

In the Confession there is not a word to show that Saint Patrick had brothers and sisters. But on this subject the monks seem to have been quite inventive, placing on the family roll of Calpurnius a list of descendants long enough to supply two or three kingdoms with bishops, priests, monks and nuns. One sister was carried to Ireland and became the mother of seventeen bishops! Another counted among her sons four bishops and three priests; she was Limania, whose eldest son was Sechnall, a bishop, and the youngest, Lugna, a priest. There was perhaps a Sechnall or Secundinus, who wrote a poem upon the life of St. Patrick, one of the most ancient in existence. But who his mother was none can tell.

A few years since, Dr. George Petrie* found on the "Island of the Religious Foreigner," in the

* Round Towers and Ecclesiastical Architecture of Ireland, by George Petrie, p. 162; Todd's St. Patrick, p. 365.

county of Galway, Ireland, a tomb-stone whose date can scarcely be later than the beginning of the sixth century. On it is this Celtic inscription: *Lie Lugnaedon Macclmene*—"The stone of Lugna, son of Limania." Perhaps it was raised over the grave of a nephew of Saint Patrick. He may have been a native of Britain, gone as a Culdee missionary to Ireland, had his cell on the little island, and there died; whence the place was called "the Isle of the Religious Foreigner." For this there is one fossil fact, a mere name on a gravestone, which happens to agree with a line in a legend. But for the rest we have only fables, and Tillemont was safe in rejecting them all.

The small boats which carried the young Patrick and his companions, with a weight of spoils, would be likely to make land at some near point. Leaving the Firth of the Clyde, a straight course west would bring them upon the Antrim coast, just where tradition fixes the landing. This tends to show that the capture was not in Gaul, but at Alcluyd. It appear that Patrick was first sold to four brothers. Fiacc's hymn runs:

> "He was called Cathraige,
> For he served four families." *

* Latin version by Colgan.

One of these brothers is said to have been Milchu, a savage master, a cruel king of Dalaradia, and a Druid. Not liking the joint-stock arrangement, and greatly pleased with the faithfulness of the slave, he bought the shares of his brothers and became sole possessor. Patrick might well prefer to serve one master rather than four, even if the one was a tyrant.

At this point we have light from the Confession. It shows that Patrick was sent daily into the fields to herd cattle; that he watched them by night, in the rain, in the snows, and all the year long, and that these severe trials were to him a means of grace. He remembered happier days. He thought upon his sins. He felt that he was far from Christ, the true home of his soul. He recalled the teachings of God's servants, and the lessons learned in his father's house. The seed of truth, long buried in his heart, sprang up and grew. Not in vain had he been devoted to the Lord in his infancy, and taught how to pray; not in vain were his parents' prayers still renewed and ascending to the Great High Priest, who was touched with the feeling of their infirmities and his bitter endurances.

"After I had come to Ireland," he says in the Confession, "I was employed every day in tending sheep; and I used to stay in the woods and on the mountain. I prayed frequently. The love and the fear of God and faith increased so much, and the spirit of prayer so grew within me, that I often prayed an hundred times in the day, and almost as often in the night. I frequently rose to prayer in the woods before daylight, in snow, and frost, and rain; and I felt no evil, nor was there any sloth in me; for, as I now see, the Spirit was burning within me.

"And there the Lord opened my unbelieving mind, so that, even late, I thought of my sins, and my whole heart was turned to the Lord my God, who looked down upon my low condition, had pity on my youth and ignorance, and preserved me before I knew him, and before I knew good from evil, and guarded, protected and cherished me, as a father would a son. This I certainly know, that before God humbled me I was like a stone lying deep in the mire; but when he came, who had all power to do it, he raised me in his mercy and put me on a very high place. Wherefore I must testify aloud, in order to make some return to the Lord for such great blessings, in time and in eternity, which no human reason is able to estimate."

Such was the experience of young Patrick; religion with him was deep heart-work. Its power came from the Lord; the Holy Ghost imparted the love and fear of God. Such was his account of his conversion, written in his old age. How he remembered those first convictions of sin and helplessness, the earnestness of those first prayers, the ardour of that first love, and all that blessedness! He drew the portrait of a new convert without intending it. How much does it reveal! If a painting by Raphael tells us the state of art among the Italians in his time, does not Saint Patrick's description of his own experience tell us what religion was held to be in his days by the Irish Christians? It was not ritual, but spiritual; not a matter of forms, but of faith; not penance, but repentance; not saint-worship, but the grateful adoration of God; not priest-work, but heart-work; not a mere reform of the conduct, but a regeneration of the soul. Surely he was never the man that thousands of his adorers believe him to have been! That portrait would never have been drawn by a papist. The young man whom it represented, and the old man who drew it, were the same Patrick; and surely he never believed that a church must confer the salvation of Christ—that God's grace and Spirit must come through the hands of a priest! To what confessional did he go in the wilderness but that only one of God, the mercy-seat, the throne of grace? That was ever near him amid the rain, the snow, and the darkness. To whom could he go but unto Him who had the words of eternal life?

"Such words as these," says D'Aubigné, "from the lips of a swineherd* in the green pastures of Ireland, set clearly before us the Christianity which in the fourth and fifth centuries converted many souls in the British Isles. In after years Rome established the dominion of priests and salvation by forms, independently of the dispositions of the heart; but the primitive religion of these celebrated islands was that living Christianity whose substance is the grace of Jesus Christ, and whose power is the grace of the Holy Ghost. The herdsman from the banks of the Clyde was then undergoing those experiences which so many evangelical Christians in those countries have since undergone. Evangelical faith, even then, existed in the British Islands in the person of this slave, and of some few Christians born again, like him, from on high."

* Quoting Ussher: *porcorum pastor erat.*

CHAPTER III.

THE ESCAPE.

SIX years wore away, but there seemed to be no promotion for Patrick. Twenty-two years of age, vigorous and enterprising, he thought of being something else than a herdsman. A heavenly Father's correction had wakened him from his sleep of death to a higher life; the great Shepherd had a nobler work for him to do. He began to have dreams, as so many of God's servants have had in all ages, wondering what they meant, and whether a divine hand and voice were in them. It will not appear strange to most Christians that several of his dreams are recorded in the Confession. Those who choose may treat them as legends, unworthy of credit; he seems to have thought they came from God.

One night, as he tells us, he seemed to hear a voice saying, "Thy fasting is well; thou shalt soon return to thy country." He waited, watched, but no way of return appeared. Again he dreamed, and the same voice said, "Behold, the ship is ready for you." But he was told that it was far distant.* He did not feel bound to go to his master, tell him all, settle up affairs, shake hands and bid him farewell. If the cruel chief found that his favourite slave was missing some morning, he must make the best of it. The Lord was recovering his stolen property. "I took to flight," he informs us, "and left the man with whom I had been for six years. I went in the power of the Lord, who directed my way for good, and I feared nothing until I came to the place where the ship lay. The ship was then clearing out, and I asked for a passage in her. The master of the vessel became angry and said, "Do not pretend to come with us." On hearing this I retired, for the purpose of going to the cabin where I had been received as a guest,† and while going thither I began to pray. But before I had finished my prayer, I heard one of the men crying out to me, "Come back quickly, for these men are calling you." I

---

* "Two hundred miles," is the present reading in the Book of Armagh. But it is supposed to be an error of the transcriber. The scholiast on Fiacc's Hymn has it, "Sixty miles, or, as others says, a hundred," a proof that there were various readings or traditions.—*Todd's St. Patrick*, p. 367.

† Or "to the hut where I used to dwell," at the risk of being ill-treated by his master.—*Tillemont*.

returned at once. They said to me, "Come, for we receive you in faith; make friends with us, as you please!"

He was surprised to hear them speak of faith, for he saw that they were heathens, but he hoped they meant to say, "Come in the faith of Jesus Christ," or he hoped that they might come over to the faith of Christ. He went with them. They were three days* at sea, probably making for the coast of Scotland. The sea must have been rough, the course lost, the harbour missed and the vessel driven upon some desolate shore. For twenty-eight days they "wandered in a desert;" a region laid waste by the ravages of the warlike tribes, or from which pirates had caused the natives to flee. They ran short of provisions. Patrick seems to have spoken to the sailors of the power of God, of prayer and of trust in his providence. Want would impress the lesson.

"What sayest thou, Christian?" asked the leader of the party. "Thy God is great and all-powerful.

---

* Dr. Lanigan brings Patrick from Dalaradia, full two hundred miles, to Bantry Bay, thence in three days to the coast of Gaul. He gives credit to a story that the fugitive had been seized by a wild Irishman and sold to certain sailors or merchants of Gaul.—*Eccl. Hist.*, i. 150. The legends bandy him about as a slave and captive most wonderfully.

Why, then, canst thou not pray to him for us? For we perish with hunger, and can find here no inhabitants."

"Turn ye in faith to my Lord God, to whom nothing is impossible," Patrick replied, "and he will send you food, for he has abundance everywhere." Soon they came upon a herd of swine; they slew, ate, rested and remained in that place for two nights. "After this," he says, "they gave thanks to God and I was honoured in their eyes." When some wild honey was found, one of the sailors offered Patrick a part of it, saying, "This is an offering, thanks to God!" But he refused it, suspecting that the man had some superstitious notions in his mind, or had offered it to a heathen god.

The same night an event occurred which he could never forget. He must have had a night-mare; he thought it a temptation of Satan. " I felt as if a great stone had fallen upon me. I could not move a limb. How it came into my mind to call out *Helias* [or Eli] I know not; but at that moment I saw the sun rising in the heavens, and whilst I cried out *Helias! Helias!* with all my might, lo, the brightness of the sun fell upon me, and straightway removed all the weight."

This has been considered "a sufficient proof"* that in his earlier days Saint Patrick invoked the saints. But it is no proof at all. Even if he called upon Elias, he says that he knew not how it came into his mind. It was something unusual; it was not his habit in youth; he could not explain how it happened in his old age. Moreover, Elias was never invoked as a saint in the Roman Church before the fourteenth century, nor in the Greek before the tenth. In some of the more ancient "Lives" the word is not "Helias" but "Eli." It may have stood thus in the original copy of the Confession, as Dr. Todd suggests.†

But what did Patrick mean by "Eli?" If he knew the gospels, he must have remembered the Saviour's loud cry, when on the cross. Without knowing what it meant, he may have used it in his strange distress. But the name Eli, "my God," was sometimes applied to Christ in the early centuries, as in the hymn of Hilary of Poictiers. Patrick might have heard it thus used before he was a captive. When in trouble he may have uttered it; he "knew not how it came into his mind." He was not accustomed to invoke God by that name in

---

* Lanigan, Carew.
† Todd's St. Patrick, pp. 370-373.

his prayers. No miracle is described. He cried aloud, and just then the sun was rising. The spell was gone. But he long afterward believed that God showed him mercy at that time. No saint had helped him. He says, "I am persuaded that I was relieved by Christ my Lord, and that his Spirit then cried out for me, and I trust it may be so in the day of my trouble, for the Lord saith in the gospel, 'It is not ye that speak, but the Spirit of your Father, which speaketh in you!'"* When he was so nearly asleep, and so benumbed that he did not think of calling upon his God, the Spirit prompted him to pray. This may be his meaning. We have dwelt upon this, because it is the only instance in the Confession which can be wrested to support the invocation of the saints.

For sixty days Patrick wandered about with the sailors. This gave rise to the story of a second captivity;† perhaps he so regarded it. It is evident that he grew weary of his company, for he says that on the sixtieth night (after leaving his

---

* Matthew x. 20.

† Probus, the Bollandists, and others. Neander represents him as carried away again from his home by pirates, and "after sixty days" restored to liberty.—*Mem. Ch. Life*, p. 426.

master, probably) "the Lord delivered me from their hands." The accounts of his wanderings on the French coasts, converting the mariners, going home with them and converting their countrymen, travelling about in Europe and ever drifting Romeward, have not a shadow of foundation in the Confession. It goes on to say: "After a few years [of absence in captivity] I was again with my parents in Britain,* who received me as a son, and earnestly besought me never to leave them again, after having endured such great tribulations."

The Clyde, the great rock, the few lingering Roman soldiers—and the home of his youth had no longer any power to retain him in his native land. To prove himself a real Succath, "strong in war," and make himself a captain fearful in Pictish eyes, was not to his mind. He had other thoughts. Loving them still, he could leave father and mother for the sake of Christ. When he slept he saw Ireland in visions, and heard the voices of its youth calling upon him to hasten and help them. Of his dream he says, "In the dead of night I saw a man coming to me as if from Ireland, whose

† Brittaniis. Villanueva reads, "Britannia." Bede used the plural form, for Britain was divided into several parts.

name was Victor,* bearing innumerable epistles. And he gave me one of them, and I read the beginning of it, which contained the words, 'The voice of the Irish.' And while repeating them, I imagined that I heard in my mind the voice of those who were near the wood of Foclut, which is near the Western Sea. Thus they cried, 'We pray thee, holy youth, to come and henceforth walk among us.' I was pierced in heart, and could read no more; and so I awoke. Thanks be to God, that after very many years the Lord granted unto them the blessing for which they cried!

"Again on another night—I know not, God knoweth, whether it was within me or near me, I heard distinctly words which I could not understand, except these at the close: 'He who gave his life for thee is he who speaketh in thee.' And so I awoke rejoicing." In some of his dreams he was led to recall such texts of Scripture as these: "The Spirit helpeth our infirmities." "Christ, who maketh intercession for us." If such was the effect of his dreaming, it was not in vain. There

---

* This *man* Victor is called an angel in the "Lives" written by Saint Patrick's adorers. The name is given to his supposed guardian angel. What he relates as a dream they represent as a reality. What he "imagined" they make miraculous.

is nothing here absurd. All is quite consistent with the feelings of a man who is enthusiastic and eager to tell the good news of salvation to a barbarous people. We should not forget his object in telling these dreams. It was to show that he did not assume the ministry of his own accord. He was not sent by men. He felt that he was called of God. If he thought that his call was supernatural, and that there was something more than imagination in his visions, it was only what many other excellent men have thought concerning their own dreams. Rightly or wrongly, he took them as signs that he was commissioned by the Lord to preach the gospel in Ireland.

Is it at all likely that he spent thirty-five years in studies and travels before returning to Ireland? Is it likely that he waited until he was sixty years of age before preaching anywhere? Did he roam about from the year 395 to the year 432, now studying with Martin of Tours, now at the renowned monastery at Lerins, and again at Rome? And all this time dreaming of Ireland, and thinking that God was calling him to the work? It can hardly be credited. But we may well suppose that he studied for several years in the best school that he could afford.

CHAPTER IV.

THE FAILURES OF PALLADIUS.

WHILE Patrick is preparing for his work in Ireland, let us see how far the field is prepared for him. We shall thus understand that some efforts of his predecessors were afterward ascribed to him in order to increase his glory.

It is, to this day, the boast of every true Irishman that Erin was never invaded by the Romans —the Cæsars gained no footing there. Its brave, warlike, hospitable, high-minded people detested the idea of being a mere province of the great empire. They appear to have sent boat-loads of heroes across the Channel to aid their brethren, the Scots, against the foreign army on the Clyde. Hating Roman soldiers, would they love Roman missionaries? It might have been hard for even a Briton to gain a hearing among them.

Who first taught the gospel in Ireland has never been shown to the people of our days. It may be putting the case too boldly to say that " the Church of Lyons and that of Ireland were both founded by Greeks, and the Scotch and Irish clergy long spoke no other tongue."* O'Halloran, a Romanist, says: "I strongly suspect that by Asiatic or African missionaries, or through them by Spanish ones, were our ancestors instructed in Christianity, because they rigidly adhered to their customs as to tonsure and the time of Easter. Certain it is that Patrick found a hierarchy established in Ireland." As to the "hierarchy" there is no evidence. The very notion of one, before Patrick, is stoutly opposed by other Roman Catholic historians. "It is certain," says Father Brenan, "that there was neither a hierarchy nor a Christian bishop in Ireland antecedent to the period of which we are treating (431), although it is highly probable that the natives, in many parts of the island, were by no means unacquainted with the Christian religion."†

No doubt at an early day there were in the southern part of Ireland "some few Christian families, separated from each other, and probably ignorant of each other's existence. . . . It cannot be denied that the traditions of Irish Church

---

* Michelet, Hist. of France, ch. iii.
† Brenan's Eccl. Hist. of Ireland, ch. i.

SAINT PATRICK.

history speak of isolated congregations of Christians in Ireland before the arrival of Patrick."*
They are to be counted among "the Scots believing on Christ" before Palladius was sent to them as their "first bishop," as a bishop was then held to be at Rome. The case will be cleared if we assume that their teachers and ministers were Culdees—that in many a quiet place was a cell, and the simple-hearted people gathered to hear the Word and worship God.

The affairs of "the infant Church" of Ireland began to be talked of at Rome, where Celestine was chief bishop, and the error was gaining strength that he was the high pontiff of all the churches in the world. The Christians of Ireland ought to acknowledge him as "the holy father" and pope! What a blessing to them, if they only knew it! The gospel might be with them, but the orders of clergy were wanting. They might have Christ, but they had not the Church in its latest and most improved form. They had followed the simple apostles, but were far behind the wise fathers. They might have presbyters, but they had no high prelate—not even "a bishop!"

Celestine was moved "by the increasing number

* Todd's St. Patrick, pp. 189, 221.

of Christians there,"* to act as a father toward "the infant Church" of the remote island. He would knit ties between it and the Church of Rome. Those artless Christians should have all the benefit of the improvements invented by men, who saw in the great Roman empire their model for Christendom, and who constructed offices in the Church to correspond with the offices in the State. They should have a bishop, a sort of church pro-consul, or resident legate—one who would not merely look after the sheep, but hold a general rule over the shepherds. He cast his eye about on his clergy to find a proper man. He wished to send him, not to the heathen Irish, but to "the Scots† believing on Christ," and yet, "whose faith was not right;" not to be a missionary, but a ruler; not merely to preach, but to use power; not to convert the ignorant so much as to confirm the believers in the gospel according to Rome; not to bring the pagans unto Christ, so much as to bring Christians under the Roman Church.

Among the men of promise and zeal was Pal-

* Moore's Hist. Ireland, p. 209.

† The Scots of Ireland as well as of Scotland. Thackeray supposes that Patrick requested Celestine to send a bishop to Ireland.—*Anc. Brit.* ii. 166.

ladius. There is small proof that he was a native of Britain and a deacon of the Church of Rome. It seems clearer that he was quite sound in doctrine, holding with Augustine the great truths of man's native depravity, inability to save himself and need of Christ's atonement and power. He was grieved to see the errors of Pelagius taking root in the British Isles—errors growing out of the denial of man's sinfulness by nature, and leading fallen sinners to think that they could save themselves by their own moral works. He wished some strong defender of the faith to be sent to Britain, in answer to a loud call from that quarter for the aid of some defender of the truth. Perhaps he had some part in sending Germanus in his own stead, to displace the heretics and direct the Britons to the Catholic faith."* Perhaps it was he who told Celestine also of the believers in Ireland "whose faith was not right." Their error, however, was not Pelagianism.

Here was the man to place over the Christians of Ireland. He was raised to a bishop, and A.D. 431 sent forth by Celestine,† with a goodly array

* Prosper's Chronicle. Ussher's Brit. Eccl. Antiq.

† "France was probably the country from which Palladius and his companions came; and the mission to Ireland, of

of attendants. He went thinking that those "believers greatly needed the unity which a bishop alone could give them." Of course some of the Romish historians relate that Patrick was chosen to attend Palladius. Of course they represent the bishop as carrying with him, not only a copy of the Sacred Scriptures, but also "a portion of the relics of St. Peter and St. Paul!"

Palladius thus appears as "an emissary of the Roman See, whose object was to organize Christianity among the Scots of Ireland and Scotland, in accordance with what was then the Roman model. The civil power of Rome being on the wane, the ecclesiastical power began to rise on its ruins, and there may have been no little connection between the two processes; the loss of one species of power may have helped an ambitious people, accustomed to universal dominion, to seek after the establishment of another."*

On the Wicklow coast he landed, but he was not well received. Why not? An old Irish chronicler says of him: "He was sent to convert

which he was the head, although sanctioned by the See of Rome, was in reality projected and sent forth by the Gallican Church."—*Todd's St. Patrick*, p. 280.

* McLauchlan, Early Scot. Ch. p. 88.

this island, lying under wintry cold, but God hindered him, for no man can receive anything from earth unless it be given him from heaven; for neither did those fierce and savage men receive his doctrine readily, nor did he himself wish to spend time in a land not his own."

It appears that he began to preach "in the country of the Hy Garchon," but their prince, Nathi, took offence, and ordered him to leave. Palladius had not the zeal needed to force his opinions and make converts, nor the courage of which heroes and martyrs are made, or he had such tenderness toward the native Christians that he did not wish to bring trouble upon them. Some tell us that he was driven back by the violence of the barbarians; others, that " he paraded his authority before the Christians and pagans of the island, and excited the opposition of both; and after vain efforts to subdue them to the authority of his master on the Tiber, he was compelled to abandon his design and flee the country."* The enmity of a heathen chieftain may have been one cause of the failure. " But the Roman missionary might also have to thank his own uncompromising opposition to the prejudices of those Christian communities, who are

* Ireland and the Irish. By Kirwan, *N. Y. Observer*, 1855.

mentioned as the sole object of this visit, and whose co-operation, undoubtedly, was necessary for the success of any endeavours to Christianize their pagan neighbours."* These artless followers of Christ did not want such a bishop over them. They let him know it, and regarded it as sheer impertinence for him or his master to interfere with their simple rites and their independence. The tradition is, that he founded three small churches in Ireland, in one of which he placed the "relics of the apostles" that he had carried with him!

It is curious to find the name Patricius, or Patrick, given to him by some of the oldest Irish writers. He was thus called in Ireland for centuries. It is an important fact. It has caused very much of the confusion in the accounts of Saint Patrick. Events in the life of the one have been carried over into the life of the other, thus robbing Palladius to pay Patrick. This will furnish us with a key to certain legends soon to be noticed. Palladius did not go back in despair the way whence he came. There were other "Scots believing in Christ" to be visited. An ancient writer tells us that on leaving the people who had rejected him, " he was forced to go round the coast

* Soames' Latin Church in Anglo-Saxon Times, p. 53.

of Ireland toward the north, until, driven by a great tempest, he reached the extreme part of *Modhaidh* [Mearns?], toward the south, where he founded the church of Fordoun, and *Pledi* is his name there." But Fordoun is not in the south of Scotland; it is in the north-east, not far from Aberdeen. Nor is it in the ancient land of the Scots, but in that of the Picts, where a Roman camp had been established. Did the Scots refuse to accept him as their bishop? Did he then go among the Picts and found a church? Did he there lay aside his official dignities and work as a missionary? His name seems to have become somewhat popular at that place. The church and a neighbouring well were dedicated to him. He may have proved himself an enterprising man, devoting his energies to the good of the people, in temporal matters as well as spiritual. To this day in that town an annual market is called Palladie's fair, or " Pady fair, after Palladius himself."* This goes to show that he lived there for years, rather than a few months. To make the end of his mission suit the beginning of Saint Patrick's, it has been usual to fix his death at March 16, 432, not perhaps a year after his first landing in Ireland. This looks like shortening his

* Anc. Ch. Scot. in Spottiswoode Miscellany, p. 468.

ministry for the express benefit of the "apostle of Ireland." The story that "he was crowned with martyrdom" may be only a smoother way of saying that foul work was made with the facts of his life.

More sacredly is his life treated by the Scottish traditions. Longer space is given to it. There was no temptation to shorten his days and erase his deeds. He seems to have had some disciples, who became eminent missionaries. One of them was Servanus. The story* is that he was a native Scot, " lived according to the forms and rites of the primitive Church" until the coming of Palladius. "The holy Servanus" was attracted to the new bishop;† he received instruction; he aided in teaching the people "the orthodox faith," and the right form of the Church; he taught the Christian law to the clergy; and Palladius raised him to the dignity of a bishop. All this could not well have been done in a few weeks or months. The date is supposed to be 440. If Servanus founded the institution on the little isle of Loch Levin, as has

* In the Breviary of Aberdeen. It is Romish authority, and favours the Culdee theory.

† "Scotland had never before seen a bishop, and was in a state of extreme barbarism." Milner, Ch. Hist. Cent. V. ch. xi. The want of such bishops was hardly the cause or the proof of the alleged barbarity.

been claimed for ages, he would seem not to have departed very far from the Culdee system. He still had his island cell. There grew up a Culdee establishment, which stoutly resisted the advances of Rome until the twelfth century.

Another disciple was Ternanus, a Scot by birth, of noble blood, and baptized by Palladius. "If it be true that he baptized Ternanus when a child, as it is said he did, and ordained him at last bishop of the Picts, he must have lived a good while; and indeed Polydore Virgil, in his history of England, brings him down to the reign of Constantine. . . . in the year 457."* If Ternanus was baptized in adult age, and made a bishop within a few months after Palladius came, the one must have been a good and wise Christian for years, or the other a very poor and imprudent overseer of the Church. This ordination must have taken place at a much later day than 432, when those who glorify Saint Patrick hasten Saint Palladius into his grave. These accounts lead us to believe that Palladius lived and laboured several years in Scotland, and died at Fordoun, where his tomb was rifled at a later day, and his relics preserved until

* Spottiswoode Miscellany, 466. Biographie Universelle puts his death at A. D. 450.

the time of the Reformation.* True, these are traditions; they are found in records of the Middle Ages; but they are quite as well founded as the story about Saint's Patrick's commission from Rome to succeed the deceased Palladius. There is more reason to believe that Palladius lived beyond the year 432 than that Patrick took up his commission in the same year, and went as "the second bishop" to the Scots in Ireland. There is not the slightest evidence that the death of the one had any connection with the mission of the other.

What if Palladius did not die in 432? What if Celestine did? The latter could not appoint Saint Patrick as the successor of the former. It is worthy of notice that Celestine is the only Roman bishop who is said to have given his sanction to the missionary.

* Ussher, Brit. Eccl. Antiq. cap. xvi., Spott. Miss. 466.

CHAPTER V.

SIFTING THE LEGENDS.

THE tares of fable are not to be bound up with the wheat of history. To set forth the true Saint Patrick from the fabulous, we notice some of the mavellous tales that have been told of him. None of them were written during his time: they were invented after he had been several hundred years in his grave. His Romish biographers of this day are quite ashamed to repeat the most ridiculous of them. But yet they give us the thread on which they are strung, and call it history. By sifting a few of the legends we may the better know the real man from the myth of the monks.

The sum of these legends is as follows: After Patrick had received the vision of an angel calling him to Ireland, he went to Germanus for advice. Germanus had been a lawyer, a soldier and a military commander, fond of rough life, a noted hunter, and accustomed to slay wild beasts and hang their heads on a tree in the public square of

Auxerre. It was a heathen custom. It displeased the bishop, Amator, who had the tree cut down, and for this was driven from the town by the commander. But it was revealed to Amator that his enemy should one day become bishop of Auxerre. This was coming to pass, and Germanus was a layman in the Church and a general in the army when Patrick visited him on the banks of the Yonne in the heart of France. There he studied four years; some say thirty! Fiacc says of Patrick,

> "He traversed the whole of Albion,
> He crossed the sea—it was a happy voyage;
> He took up his abode with Germanus,
> Far away to the south of Amorica."

Then he went to Tours, where he passed four years with Martin, the bishop, who is represented as his uncle on the mother's side. It was important to connect him with this great man in the Western Church, who did so much to advance the claims and the glory of Rome. There his head was shorn; the tonsure marked him as one of the lower clergy. Then he grew wise in "church discipline," and learned to convert flesh into fish!

His guardian-angel does not lose sight of him. He commands the young Patrick to pass some time with "the people of God," that is, the barefoot hermits in some retired corner of the world, which they thought was quite out of it. With them he lingers eight years, and becomes a quite passable monk. Thence he is sent by the angel to visit certain islanders in the "Tyrrhene Sea." He finds three other Patricks in a solitary cave, and asks leave to dwell with them. They answer that he cannot unless he will draw water from a certain fountain which is guarded by a very savage wild beast. He agrees to this. He goes to the fountain. The ravenous beast sees him; gives signs of great joy, and becomes "quite tame and gentle." Patrick draws the water and returns with a blessing. The four Patricks dwell together for nine years.* Perhaps the Romanists lost the true one there, and have followed the wrong one in the various rambles which they record! The more sober version of this part of the story is that Patrick the Briton studied for some time in the celebrated monastery at Lerins, to which he was sent by Lupus, the bishop of Troyes.†

Again the angel appears, saying, "Go to St. Senior, a bishop who is in Mount Hermon, on the south side of the ocean, and his city is fortified

* Vita Tertia, in Colgan.
† Soames, Latin Church ; Carew, Eccl. Hist. Ireland.

with seven walls." He understands better than we do the angel's geography. He goes, for nothing is easier than for him to travel great distances. Here he is ordained a priest. Here come to him the voices of the children in Ireland, entreating him to hasten and teach them. "Go to Ireland" is the angel's command.

"I cannot," he replied, "because bad men dwell there."

"Go," is the word again.

"I cannot unless I see the Lord." Patrick goes forth with nine men, and sees the Lord, who takes him to his right hand and declares to him,

"Go thou to Ireland, and there preach the word of eternal life."

"I ask of thee three petitions," answered Patrick—"that the men of Ireland be rich in gold and silver; that I may be their patron; and that, after this life, I may sit on thy right hand in heaven." (Surely this is not our Patrick!)

"Patrick, thou shalt have what thou hast asked; and, moreover, whosoever shall commemorate thee by day or by night shall not perish for ever."

He then goes to Ireland as a priest. But the people refuse to listen to him, for he has no commission from Rome. It is not enough that the

Lord has sent him. He must have a different authority. Not Heaven, but Rome, must send him, before he can have any success! He suspects the cause of his defeat, and prays to the Lord: "Who didst guide my path through the Gauls and Italy unto these islands, lead me, I beseech thee, to the holy see of the Roman Church, that I may thence receive authority to preach thy word with faithfulness, and that the people of Hiberni may by me be made Christians."* (What impiety! Is not the hand of a monk in all this?)

Patrick then sets out for Rome. On his way he again visits Germanus, and is further schooled into habits of monkish devotion. The angel urges him to go back to Ireland; he starts, and Germanus sends with him Segetius the presbyter. Not yet is he a bishop, for Palladius had been sent with that rank to the Irish. At Emboria he is met by the former companions of Palladius, and they tell him Palladius is dead. He then turns aside to "a man of wondrous sanctity, a chief bishop, named Amator (or Amatorex), dwelling in a neighbouring place," and by him Patrick is consecrated a bishop. Upon this he quickly takes ship, and reaches the unfriendly shores of the Emerald Isle. His

* Probus, quoted by Todd, St. Patrick, 324-326.

labours are successful. But in this story there is nothing of his having been at Rome, nor of a commission from "the pope." The genius of Probus was clouded in regard to the Roman mission. Of that invention he seems not to have been aware.

But we have not yet reached the climax of monkish fable. We have left out something, which we could not weave into the foregoing account. It is this: On one of his many visits to Germanus he is thus advised: "Go to the successor of St. Peter, namely Celestine, that he may ordain thee, for this office belongs to him." Patrick goes, but Celestine gives him no honour, because he has already sent Palladius to Ireland. One bishop to that country is all that he can afford. After this repulse Patrick goes with Segetius to an island in "the Tyrrhene Sea." [One version is that he took this island on his way to Rome.] There he comes to a house which seems to be new. There the master, who appears to be a very young man, points him to a very old woman, and says, "She is my daughter's granddaughter!" And much more quite as wonderful. Those who appear youngest are the oldest on that blessed isle. They had been in the habit of showing hospitality to every traveller passing that way. One night a pilgrim had come with a staff in his hand, and they had a precious relic which had the power of preserving those who sacredly kept it in all the freshness of youth. He was lodged with all kindness. In the morning he told them that he was the Lord Jesus, and leaving the staff with them, said, "Keep it safely. After a long time a certain pilgrim will come named Patrick;* give it to him." Then Patrick refused to take the staff, unless he should receive it from the Lord himself. Three days afterward he went with these remarkable people to Mount Hermon in the neighbourhood, and there it was given to him to qualify him for the conversion of Ireland. He went again to Rome [it was the first time, according to some], and was received with favour, for Celestine had now heard of the death of Palladius. He was then ordained a bishop, given the name of Patrick, and sent on the great mission, with a fair supply of relics, which, as some will have it, he filched from the pope. Three choirs then sang praises—

* The author of this wretched story forgot to represent this name as afterward given to him by "Pope Celestine," when he received his commission. The staff figures largely in the Romish lives of Saint Patrick. The pretended relic was long kept, but publicly burned at the Reformation.

one in heaven; another in Rome, and a third in the wood of Erin, where the children were still calling for "the saint" to come and bless them.* What their ages were is not told, but Patrick's is set down at sixty! He had passed nearly forty years in study and in the chase after the true Church! Verily some of our modern brethren may take courage; they are not likely to have a rougher time than had this mythical Saint Patrick in getting to Rome.

Such are the stories. Modern Romanists tone down the absurdities, and out of these trifling legends weave the accounts of Patrick's studies on the Continent and his commission from the pope. What truth is there in them? None whatever, we believe, so far as Saint Patrick is concerned. The greater part are incredible; the rest untrue. We have passed over some of the contradictions and absurdities. We may sift out a few items of apparent fact, but they seem to belong to the life of Palladius. He is the Patrick who was connected with Germanus. He may have been a disciple of Martin of Tours, and studied at Lerins. He may have been ordained by Amatorex. He may have wandered about the Mediterranean islands.

* Vita Septima, in Colgan; Joceline's St. Patrick.

He seems to have been at Emboria, wherever that was, for it is mentioned in connection with his name. He appears to have been urged by Germanus to go to Ireland, and it was he who went as a bishop, with the seal of Celestine on his commission. One account is that Saint Patrick was sent with Germanus into Britain, in 429, to suppress the Pelagian heresy; this is far more likely to have been true of Palladius, for he was zealous on that subject. The story of Patrick's repulse by the Irish is clearly borrowed from Palladius. We shall find the one represented as following closely in the footsteps of the other, landing on the same coast and driven away by the same Hy Garchon.

There is but one point where a fact seems to crop out through the mass of fables. It is where Saint Patrick is sent to Ireland in his younger days, and, as a priest or presbyter, begins his work without having been at Rome, and without any sort of commission from her bishop. It was not necessary to have a permission from that quarter. Good men and churches and synods had the right to send missionaries wherever they chose, without a word from "the holy father." Even he did not claim that all success depended upon him. He was not yet a full-blown pope. With all his faults,

Celestine was too good a bishop to assume such high powers. "A ray of truth has here broken out through clouds of fable, and no greater proof can be desired that the Roman mission was a modern addition to the facts of history."*

And yet it is assumed that St. Patrick was sent forth from Rome, as her bishop, her legate, her apostolic nuncio! Hear Father Brenan: "Upon the death of Palladius, Patrick received the regular missionary powers from the sole divinely established source of spiritual jurisdiction on earth, the head of the Church, at that time also Pope Celestine;" and thus other Romish writers assert in shorter words, from Fiacc's Scholiast down to Montalembert. It is made the great point with them. It lies at the basis of all the wonders done by "the apostle of Ireland." Without it he is nothing in their eyes. It has become deeply rooted in the hearts of thousands of Irishmen. It has made him their patron saint; they swear by his name, pray to him, adore him, and regard him as the guardian of the whole Irish race wherever they may roam in other lands.

Moreover, this Roman mission is made the central point in all the chronology of his life. All

* Todd's St. Patrick, p. 327.

other dates are conformed to it. If he was commissioned by Celestine as the successor of Palladius, it must have been in 432, for this Roman bishop died early in that year. If he was then sixty years of age, he was born in 372. But what of the other dates? If he was thirty when he went to Germanus, he must have found a poor teacher of theology, for this man was a military officer at that time, if not a heathen sportsman; he was not a bishop earlier than 418. Did Patrick study with him thirty years? When, then, did he study with Martin of Tours, who died about 402? The greenest grave of the most learned man would not be a fit place to study "church discipline." His death is fixed about the year 494, giving him the full age of one hundred and twenty-two years. These are a few of the beauties of monkish arithmetic. To fix his birth at 387 does not clear up the difficulties. These dry dates show a plentiful watering of the facts in the life of the missionary.

Was Saint Patrick ever at Rome? Perhaps he was, but there is no good evidence of it. Yet what if he were? Protestants now visit that city, and most of them come away with their faith unimpaired; so might he. And the Rome of the fifth century was not what it became in the eighth; its moon was only in the first quarter of decline and gently waning into the crescent. Her power was not the growth of one age; it was the gradual result of centuries of ambition. Even had Patrick studied there (as some legends run), and been there ordained, he might still have held none of Rome's peculiar views. Indeed, we might grant that he was sent forth, from that great centre of the empire, to labour in Ireland, and yet not admit Rome to be the mother of all the ancient churches nor the head of Christendom. The question would not be so very important if the Papists had not laid such stress upon it. "The fact that missionaries were sent out with the sanction of Rome no more proves the modern papal claim to universal supremacy, than the fact of a bishop being now sent into the interior of Africa, with the sanction of Canterbury, would prove the universal supremacy of the Primate of England."*

Was Saint Patrick sent to Ireland with a commission from Celestine? The question is important. Its answer will help to solve many difficulties. We state some of our reasons for rejecting the story of the Roman mission:

1. It is based on the legends of which we have

* Todd's St. Patrick, p. 333, *note.*

given a specimen; rather were these fables framed to support it. They are of comparatively late origin. They were put forth at a time when some show of foundation was needed for the pope's power in Ireland.

2. It is not mentioned by the older writers. This is admitted by the most candid Roman Catholic historians, who base it only on tradition.* Could an appointment of so great moment have been unknown to the chroniclers of that age? If known, would they have passed it over in silence? Yet, strange to relate, centuries seem to have rolled away before the important commission with which Saint Patrick is said to have been honoured by Saint Celestine was mentioned by any British or foreign writer.† Not a word is said about it by Sechnall, his supposed nephew, his disciple and eulogist. He wrote a poem in praise of the great man, but thrust upon him no glory derived from an education on the Continent or a sanction from Rome. He describes him as "constant in the fear of God, immovable in faith, one upon whom as a second Peter the Church is built, and one who obtained from God

* Lanigan, Colgan, Carew.
† Carew, Eccl. Hist. Ireland, p. 74.

his apostleship. The Lord chose him to teach barbarous nations, and to fish with the nets of doctrine." Fiacc's Hymn represents him as educated on the Continent, but says nothing of the Roman mission. If it were a fact, they certainly would not have ignored such an honour, unless they were too proud of the independence of the Irish Church.*

Prosper of Aquitaine took into his special care the praises of Celestine, for he was the bishop's friend and counsellor. He advised the sending of Palladius to "the Scots believing in Christ." Palladius went, stayed a few weeks, raised three chapels, and ran away; yet for this brief and ignoble effort Celestine is named with high honour. But Patrick went to Ireland, laboured there twenty-three years before Prosper finished his chronicle, and was blessed with the most signal success. Was not this to the honour of Celestine, who did not live to hear of it? Was he not the spiritual father of the Irish Church? Yet Prosper never mentions Patrick. He neither tells us that he was at Rome nor that he was sent out from Rome. Why not? It must have been for the

* Todd's St. Patrick, p. 312. This silence occurs in five of the seven lives in Colgan's Trias Thaumaturga.

reason that Celestine had no part in the glorious work of redeeming the sons of Erin to the Lord. Nor had Rome. Patrick had gone forth from another quarter, and Prosper did not care to relate the deeds of an independent missionary.

Bede maintains the like silence. He enters Patrick in his martyrology as a presbyter, which is some proof of his existence. He mentions Ninian, and Palladius, and Columba as eminent missionaries; why not Patrick? He either knew nothing of the mission to Ireland, or he cared not to tell what he knew. He could hardly have been ignorant. Was it because he could not honestly say that Patrick was in Rome, and could not in any way make him support the Roman pretensions of the eighth century? Bede had a strong love for the Roman party. The deeds of its bishops and popes he gloried in telling. But if Patrick was only a presbyter, an independent missionary, an associate of the Culdees, a humble man who had devoted himself to the Irish mission by the command of Christ, he was not thought worthy of mention.*

3. Patrick is evidently confounded with Palladius. This we have shown as a conclusion drawn

* Soames, Lat. Ch. p. 50; McLauchlan, Early Ch. Scot. p. 97.

from sifting the legends. "We infer," says Dr. Todd, "that the whole story of Patrick's connection with St. Germain and mission from Celestine should be regarded as a fragment of the lost history of Palladius, transferred to the second and more celebrated Patrick, by those who undertook to interpolate the authentic records of his life. The object of these interpolaters was evidently to exalt their hero. They could not rest satisfied with the simple and humble position in which his own writings, his confession and his letter to Coroticus had placed him. They could not concede to Palladius the honour of a direct mission from Rome, without claiming for Patrick a similar honour. They could not be content that their own Patrick should be regarded as an unlearned, a rude uneducated man, even though he has so described himself. The biography of Palladius, '*alio nomine Patricius,*' supplied them with the means of effecting their object, and gave to the interpolated story the appearance of ancient support." Thus we may account for what is related of Patrick's education on the Continent, his monastic tonsure, his ordination by Amator, his consecration by Celestine, his Roman mission and his first failure in Ireland. They belong to the first Patrick. " No ancient or trustworthy authority has countenanced these statements in reference to the second Patrick."*

This patchwork makes a chaos of chronology, as if the dates were thrown into a box, shaken up, and drawn out by one whose eyes are so bandaged that he cannot see the facts of history. We shall present, in the next chapter, a chronology that will better accord with the facts of Saint Patrick's life; but it will set at naught all theories of the Romish mission.

4. The reception and success of Saint Patrick argue against the Roman mission. If we understand that the Irish people hated civil Rome, and were suspicious of ecclesiastical Rome, all will be clear. Palladius was rejected because he came to place a new yoke upon the Irish Christians, and be their chief bishop, teaching them new usages and ruling in a new way.† Patrick went with no Roman views or commission, no aim to lord it over God's heritage, no design but to preach Christ and save sinners; and he succeeded. He bore the true cross, and not the crosier. View him as a Romish prelate, and there is confusion; regard him as an earnest Christian missionary,

* Soames, Lat. Ch. p. 50.
† Todd's St. Patrick, pp. 321, 332, et passim.

going forth from North Britain, and all is clear. Cut him loose from the meshes of Rome, and the burden of continental legends rolls away. He then stands forth a devoted minister of Christ, with a tongue that can gain the Irish ear and a soul that can win the Irish heart.

5. Saint Patrick claimed to have gone to Ireland of his own accord. None compelled him. He went "bound in the spirit," and with no call but that of the Lord. To show this fact he refers to his dreams. He had the sanction of his God and of his own conscience; he needed none from Rome.

6. There are intimations that he was ordained in Britain for the work. Certain "respectable clergymen" at first opposed his consecration, on acccount of an old fault, committed thirty years before in his youth. We have seen that some of the legends represent him as ordained in Gaul, without any connection with Rome. Such accounts would hardly be mere inventions of the monks.

7. There is not one word in his own writings about an education on the Continent, or a Roman mission, or a friendship with Martin of Tours, Germanus or Celestine. Why not? He was writing in his old age, when Rome was rising toward the papacy, and receiving more and more

honour on the Continent. He had been charged with presumption in having undertaken such a work as the conversion of the Irish, rude and unlearned as he was, and on his own authority. What a chance now for him to boast a little of his former advantages, and tell of his education abroad and of his commission from Rome! This would have settled the question of his right to preach with those who favoured the Roman pretensions. But he said nothing of the kind. We infer, then, that he had never held any connection with Rome, or that the people had prejudices in that direction which he did not wish to rouse. They may have stood firmly on the ground of their independence. They may have cared little for Roman education, and less for Roman commissions. And that after Saint Patrick had been long with them! On such matters, probably, he and they were agreed.

Even if the Confession be a forgery, this argument will hold good. For its author, assuming the name of Saint Patrick, evidently wrote with no design to prop up the theory of a Roman mission or a Continental education. He knew not their value, or he was not making up a history of events that never occurred. He so fully threw himself back into Saint Patrick's times and circumstances that he told only the truth. But here is a proof that the Confession is not a forgery. It is not stuffed with lying legends. Its very face proclaims that it was written by a man of truth, and such a man would not pen a "pious fraud." It served as a basis for the later manufacturers; they used the good material as they pleased. It was gold for their alloys. But they cared not to multiply copies of it, and few now remain in the original form. It was cast into the shade, for it could not serve the purposes of the Roman Church.*

8. We shall find that the Irish Church was not conformed to the Roman during several centuries after Saint Patrick's death. "If Patrick came to Ireland as a deputy from Rome, it might naturally be expected that in the Irish Church a certain sense of dependence would always have been preserved toward the mother Church of Rome. But we find, on the contrary, in the Irish Church afterward, a spirit of church freedom similar to that shown by the ancient British Church, which struggled against the yoke of Roman ordinances. . . . This goes to prove that the origin of this Church was independent of Rome." † To this we shall again recur

* Todd's St. Patrick, p. 387.
† Neander, Ch. Hist., p. 123.

when we consider whether Saint Patrick held any official connection with Rome, in his oversight of the Church to which he gave his toils. Some prelatists think that he committed errors in not forming dioceses, and placing "bishops" over them. His bishops were pastors, each having charge of a particular church. "The very errors into which he fell" are cited as evidence that he did not hold his appointment from Rome.*

* The Church of St. Patrick, by Rev. W. G. Todd, London, 1844, p. 30.

CHAPTER VI.

AMONG THE DATES.

AFTER clearing away the rank growth of legends from the path of Saint Patrick, we may now follow the track of his life. It is still like an old Indian trail through the dark woods; many of the trees once "blazed" have fallen, and the footprints have become dim. But here is an ancient landmark, there an outlying fact, and with cautious step we undertake to follow him from the home of his parents on the Clyde. There we left him, lately returned from his captivity.

It is expressly stated in the Irish version of Nennius* that Patrick was a slave with Milchu when Palladius was sent to Ireland. If this be true, he was a slave in the year 431. If that was the first year of his bondage, he was then sixteen; if the last, he was about twenty-two, for these are admitted to be the dates of his capture and his

* Nennius, abbot of Bangor, wrote about A.D. 688.—*Cave, Scrip. Hist. Lit.* Sæc. vii. 620; *Todd's St. Patrick,* p. 394.

release. This would give the year 409–415 as the period of his birth. As the Romanists are eager to link him with Palladius, we might assume that both of them left Ireland the same year. We see no way of bringing them together unless we suppose that the ship which bore the bishop northward was the very same that took up the fugitive young man of twenty-two. Both are said to have had rough sailing, and a wreck on the Scottish coast might have separated them for ever. Nor can we imagine how Celestine heard of Patrick, or sent him to Ireland, unless the bishop forwarded by post a report of the zeal shown by the young Briton on shipboard. Then comes the commission. Patrick gets it after one of his dreams, and with all speed departs to the children calling to him from the dark forests of Erin. We submit this theory as quite equal to any other which puts into the hands of Patrick a parchment sealed by the dying Celestine.

We take the date of Nennius as nothing more than a close guess at the truth. He had no idea of the Roman mission. Let us take other data. From some of the additions to the Confession we learn that Patrick had committed a fault, we know not what, when fifteen years of age. Thirty years afterward he was about to be fully ordained to the work of the ministry. His friends opposed his going. One of them, to whom he had confessed the old forgiven fault, brought it forward as an objection. He was overruled. This would make Patrick forty-five years of age at his ordination.

Now if we can find the date of this event, we may clear up various difficulties. Let us assume that he sought ordination to qualify him more fully for the work in Ireland. When did he go thither? A curious Irish tract says that the battle of Ocha happened exactly forty-three years after the coming of Patrick to Ireland. In this fray Oilioll Molt was slain. The annals of Ulster fix it at 482–483. This would give 440 as about the date of Patrick's mission.

By comparing Tirechan with Keating we have these dates: King Laogaire died in 474. He had reigned after the coming of Patrick thirty-two years. This gives the year 442 as the date of the mission.

An Irish bard and historian of the eleventh century* says that Pope Gregory died one hundred and sixty-two years after Patrick's coming. Gregory

* Gilla Cæmhain, quoted more fully in Todd's St. Patrick, p. 396.

died in 604. This gives 442 as the year of the mission. Dr. Todd furnishes other dates, all drawn from sources independent of each other, and varying little from those which we have quoted from his pages. Let the above suffice; we are not writing an arithmetic. We have good grounds for assuming that about 442 was the date of his mission to Ireland, that he was then forty-five years of age, and that 397 was the year of his birth.

Here then are twenty-three years which he had at his disposal after his return from captivity—a very considerable number for study and for the trial of his gifts as a preacher. But we may suppose the time well employed. We are not driven to hide him in a monastery. There are a few traces of active labours; they are mere traditions, but they accord with the circumstances of his life, and help to fill up the picture of his times.

Where did this young Briton study? Not surely at Tours with Saint Martin, for, if our dates be correct, the one was an infant when the other was lying in his grave. It may have been at some Culdee cell or college, where the Bible was the chief classic, and students were hardly trained to write Latin letters with the elegance of Cicero. He never became a scholar. His knowledge of Latin was limited. In later years he spoke of himself as a man who "was afraid to write in the language of the civilized world, because he had not read like others, who had been devoted to sacred learning from their infancy, and his speech had been changed to another tongue." He had preached and prayed in the language of the Irish people. Very modestly he acknowledged himself to be "rustic, unlearned," brought up in the country as an uneducated man. But he seems to have been an Apollos mighty in the Scriptures, and able to move his illiterate hearers by the power of his eloquence. We infer therefore that his education was scriptural rather than classical. It was like that of Ninian, who had found his views of Bible truth quite different from those taught at Rome.

Were there any ties between Patrick and Germanus of Auxerre? It is not easy to completely sever their names. They seem to have clasped hands, and that on British soil. This view is favoured by traditions not in the interest of the Romish monks. It is worthy of notice that while the one was thinking of going to Ireland as a missionary, the other was coming to Britain as the champion of the true faith. The Pelagians were busy in teaching the Britons that sin had not rendered man a helpless sinner, and that by his good works he might save himself. There were many Christians who would not accept these errors, and yet could not ably defend the truth. They asked the churches of Gaul to send them help. At a synod held in 429 Germanus was chosen to visit Britain. The armour of a spiritual warrior was upon him, but perhaps he had learned from the great Augustine that good word, "Slay the errors, but love the erring." With him went Lupus, afterward the bishop of Troyes, who was called "the prince of Gallican prelates, the rule of manners, the pillar of virtue, the friend of God, the intercessor for men with Heaven." There is no good ancient evidence that they took a commission from "Pope Celestine," yet he may have volunteered to grant them his blessing. They crossed the Channel, and probably went up through Cornwall, visited Glastonbury, and entered the valleys of Wales, preaching along the roads and in the fields. They seemed to carry everything before them. The humble Christians were delighted; the haughty errorists, so fond of giving strength to the pride of man, began to make their boasts.

A great debate was to come off at Verulam. Bede describes the scene in his lively style. He says that the champions of heresy came in gorgeous robes, while those of the truth appeared plainly dressed and diffident. "An immense multitude was assembled, with their wives and children. On the one side was divine faith; on the other, human presumption. On the one side, piety; on the other, pride. On the one side, Pelagius [by his representatives]; on the other, Christ. . . . Germanus and Lupus permitted their adversaries to speak first, who occupied a long time and filled the ear with empty sounds. Then the venerable prelates poured forth the torrent of their apostolic and evangelical eloquence. Their speeches were filled with Scripture sentences. . . . The Pelagian party, not being able to answer, confessed their errors. The people, who were judges, could scarcely be restrained from acts of violence, but signified their judgment by their acclamations." *

Germanus remained for some time in Britain. Among the wonders related of him is his part in a battle. The Scots and Picts were coming down upon the Britons. The fray bade fair to be fierce. Germanus is said to have baptized many of the

* Bede, Eccl. Hist. lib i. cap. 17.

British soldiers, and then acted quite as a general, as he well knew how to do. He probably knew the value of tremendous shouting. The fight began; he shouted *hallelujah* three times; the word ran along the line; the whole army took it up, and the enemy took fright, and retreated in the greatest disorder.* The spot in Wales where this affair is supposed to have occurred is called the Field of Garmon, the Welsh name of Germanus. Several Welsh churches bear his name. Such events were likely to draw the attention of young Patrick.

To find Patrick in Wales need not surprise us. Between the people of the two countries there were ties of language, and, probably, of religion. Thither the Highlanders were quite likely to drive many families from the lands of the Clyde. One tradition is, that Patrick had a retreat and a cell in the Vallis Rosina, which some have claimed as his birth-place. It is said, also, that he preached in Wales and Cornwall, with whose Celtic speech he might have been familiar. If this were true, he would scarcely fail to spend some time at Glastonbury, which has been called the cradle of British Christianity, "the first ground of God, the first

* Bede, Eccl. Hist. lib i. cap. 20.

ground of the saints in England; the rise and fountain of all religion in England." It was called the holy isle of Avalon. Its church claimed descent from the churches of Asia Minor. One tradition is, that Patrick studied there for thirty years; another, that he died there and was buried. His name was loved in these regions, and given to several churches. In later days the Irish Christians looked with reverence toward Glastonbury, and thither made their pilgrimages. It is possible that Germanus met Patrick at some of these points before returning to Gaul. They may have eaten together some of the famous apples of Avalon.*

William of Malmsbury says: "When Germanus was meditating a return into his native country, he formed an intimate acquaintance with Patrick, whom he sent after some years to the Irish as a preacher, at the bidding of Celestine." The latter part of this sentence we do not believe; the "some years" reveal the mistake. Celestine had but a few months to live. But the "intimate acquaintance" was very possible. Patrick may have learned much from the man of heroic zeal, who caused the churches to be thronged, and preached in the open fields, along the highways, and wher-

---

* Camden, Britannia, Col. 63.

ever he could make war against the heresies of Pelagius. They may have talked together of Ireland, whose rulers were deluded by the bards and priests of Druidism.

There are traces of other labours. "This St. Patrick did not neglect his native country of North Britain, but was very useful and assistant to the other instruments of that good work, in bringing the people into and confirming them more and more in the Christian faith."* Such is the statement of a writer in the early part of the eighteenth century, when referring to certain traditions of Scotland, where the name of Patrick sometimes appears in towns and churches.

There is no good proof that Patrick ever set foot out of the British Isles, and yet he may have crossed the Channel and laboured in Armorica. One story is, that he there passed three or four years as a pastor, under the direction of Germanus.† A Celtic Briton would not have been an entire stranger in that country of Celts, who had such a readiness to accept the gospel. It also has treasured his name and claimed his birth. He may have helped to start a movement which be-

* Anc. Ch. Scot. in Spottiswoode Miscellany.
† Lanigan, Eccl. Hist. Ireland, vol. i. 79.

came wonderful after his departure, and continued for almost a century. The Saxons were devouring Britain and driving away her Christian people. "To escape from their bloody yoke, an army of British monks, guiding an entire tribe of men and women, freemen and slaves, embarked in vessels not made of wood, but of skins sewn together, singing, or rather howling, under their full sails, the lamentations of the Psalmist, and came to seek an asylum in Armorica. . . . This emigration lasted more than a century, and threw a new but equally Celtic population into that part of Gaul which Roman taxation and barbarian invasion had injured least, and where the ancient Celtic worship had retained most vitality. With the exception of three or four episcopal cities, almost all the Armorican peninsula was still pagan in the sixth century. All the symbols and rites, the myths and arcanas of paganism seemed to be concentrated in that wild and misty country." (Yet some writers picture it as the blessed Eden that, in 372, gave Saint Patrick to the world.) The British missionaries "came to ask shelter of their brethren, issued from the same race and speaking the same language. They undertook to pay for the hospitality they received by the gift of a true faith, and they succeeded. They gave their name and worship to their new country. . . . Fifty years after their appearance the Gospel reigned in the peninsula."* If Patrick did not aid in it, he must have known of the movement when toiling among another Celtic people.

A ray of truth may have gleamed upon Probus when he said that Patrick began his work in Ireland as a young man and "a priest." In one of the supposed additions to the Confession he is made to say to certain Irish Christians, "You know, and God knoweth, how I walked among you from *my youth.*" This may mean that he began his ministry among them before he was ordained to the office of "a bishop," whatever that was. He may have laboured in the southern part of the island, where the little bands of Christians were most numerous. Wars among the tribes may have hindered him from great efforts which the chroniclers would notice. Some of them, how-

* Montalembert, Monks of the West, ii. p. 260, *et seq.;* also Gildas and Camden. The latter says "From that time the Armorici, being subdued by little and little, the name of Britains grew so great in this new country that the whole body of inhabitants began to fall under it, and the tract to be called *Britannica Armorica.*" Also D'Israeli's Amenities of Literature, ii. 2.

ever, dated his arrival about the year 436. Often he may have crossed and recrossed the Irish Channel. He may have tasted the dangers of labouring in such a country. Wishing to have full power to organize churches and ordain ministers, he may have applied for ordination in Britain. Then came the opposition of his relatives and friends.

"Why does this man rush into danger among the heathen, who know not the Lord?" they said one to another. "That fault in his youth!" whispered a confidant. But he persevered. Nothing could turn him aside—not their offers of wealth, not their tears. He was ready to leave all and follow Christ. "Many gifts were offered me with tears, if I would remain," he tells us. "I was forced to offend my relations and many of my well-wishers. But with God's guidance I did not yield to them at all, not by my own power, for it was God who triumphed in me. He did not hinder me from my labour, which I had dedicated to my Lord Christ. I felt no small power from him, and my faith was proved before God and men. Wherefore I boldly say that my conscience reproves me not here nor hereafter."

And yet so vigorous a man may have felt young

at forty-five, or he would so appear to himself when over ninety, and then looking back to the time when he fully entered upon his mission. In the prime of life he set foot on the shores of Erin as a missionary. That he went first to the tribes of Leinster, landed at Inbher Dea, on the Wicklow coast, made a few converts, roused the wrath of the Hy Garchon, yielded the ground, took ship again, and sailed northward, is extremely doubtful. It looks too much like a story borrowed from the adventures of Palladius. "It is not reasonable to suppose that both missionaries should have done exactly the same things; that both should land at the same place, both be driven off by the same chieftain, and both turn to the north of the island; with this difference only, that Palladius is driven (according to some accounts) by a storm round the northern coast of Scotland to the region of the Picts, and Patrick landed safely in Dalaradia, where his ministry is at once successful. Patrick, we may readily believe, went at once to Ulster, to visit the place with which he was formerly acquainted, and where he expected to be well received." * The oldest authorities have nothing of the Wicklow story.

* Todd's St. Patrick, p. 339, *slightly condensed.*

CHAPTER VII.

FIRST LABOURS OF PATRICK.

AN Irish herdsman is said to have kept the flocks of his master Dichu near the lower end of the Strangford Lough. One day he strolled down toward the shore, and saw a boat put into a little cove, as if there was some secret business on hand. Out of it stepped a small party of men, who had been wearied in toiling with the waves. Carefully stowing away their luggage, they hid their boat among the rushes, and then set forth to explore the country. A man of about forty-five years appeared to be the chief of the party.

"Robbers," thought the herdsman. "Pirates from the land of the Picts!" They seemed to be gazing over the neighborhood, as if spying out the land, and about to choose some house to plunder or fall upon some unguarded flock. They must have been hungry enough, if they had been for three days upon a barren isle, since called Inis Patrick, just off the Dublin coast. One story is, that they had sought to make them a home on its sands, where no man dwelt, and famine threatened their lives. Not even a fish would enter their nets, and the water-fowl took wing. The choice of such an island would indicate that they were Culdees, seeking the spot for a cell. "The practice of taking possession of secluded islands continued to characterize the Culdee system, and was carried by the missionaries, sent forth from time to time, whithersoever they went."* But the herdsman knew not the habits of Culdees, and he ran as fast as his feet could take him from the invaders. "Pirates" was the burden of every breath.

Now his master, Dichu, had a choice home, and he happened to be in at the time. He was a great man in those parts, having the blood of an ancient king in his veins, and a goodly array of clansmen on his estates. His riches would afford fine spoils for a troop of marauders. The report of his almost breathless herdsman roused his fears, his wrath and his courage. He sounded the alarm. The clansmen gathered at his call. He took his sword and they their pikes. All marched forth eager for the fray. They drew nearer to the invaders.

The chieftain was struck first, not with a "holy

* McLauchlan, Early Scot. Ch. p. 182.

staff," but with the noble bearing and frank, friendly countenance of the leader of the strange party. He had not seen a more winning face for many a day. The foot of heaven's messenger seems never before to have pressed his soil. He knew not Scripture enough to ask, "Comest thou peaceably?" It would not have cleared up the mystery for the leader to say, "I am Patrick, a missionary. In the name of the living God I come to declare to you the glad tidings of salvation. My greeting is the angel's song, 'Peace on earth, good-will to men.'" For this chieftain was a heathen. He had heard of no Druid's prophecy,* beginning thus:

> "He comes, he comes with shaven crown,
> From off the storm-tossed sea."

The sword was dropped. The warrior's face grew mild. The descendant of kings talked with the man of God. A finger pointed to the house, and a welcome was given to Patrick and his companions. It was not "a multitude of holy bishops, presbyters, deacons, exorcists, readers, door-keepers, and students," as some would have us believe. As for "some Gauls" and certain priests, who had

* The legend of such a prophecy by a pagan Druid was the manufacture of a papal monk long after the event.

packed up their robes on the banks of the Tiber, our eyes do not perceive them. Rather were they such assistants as a missionary would be likely to take with him to a heathen land. They went to the house; hospitality opened the way for the gospel. Patrick preached, the chieftain listened and believed in Christ. He was afterward baptized, and all his family. He was "the first of the Scots" who confessed the faith under the preaching of Patrick.

We may suppose that friends and neighbours were urged to come and listen to the good news which the stranger had to tell; that the house became crowded, and that the missionary led them to the barn on the lands of the chieftain. There the Word grew and believers multiplied. One day the chieftain felt his heart touched with gratitude to God. "I give you the land on which we are standing," said he to the preacher. "In place of this barn let a church be built."

"It shall be done," we hear Patrick reply, "and may God's house be your habitation."

"I only ask," said Dichu, "that the length of the church shall not be from east to west, but from north to south."

"It shall thus stand," answered the missionary,

for he did not see any virtue in having a church fronting toward the east, as was the general custom in Oriental lands. What would the Lord care for that? It was a mere trifle. The farther account is: "Then Patrick erected in that place the transverse church, which is called even to the present day, Sabhal Patraic, or Patrick's Barn." The place is now called Sabhal, or Saul, and is about two miles from Downpatrick. It appears that other churches were built after this model, extending from north to south.* Thus was established a base of operations.

The story is, that Patrick was concerned for Milchu, his former master, from whom he had run away without being redeemed by money. He set set forth on foot to visit him. He went in the very face of danger, "to offer to his former master a double ransom—an earthly one in money and worldly goods, and a spiritual one—by making known to him the Christian faith and the gospel way of salvation." Going northward into Antrim, he reached the top of a hill, where he stood gazing upon the scene of his exposures to the rains and snows of his vigils, his prayers and his dreams.

* Bingham's Eccl. Antiq. bk. viii. 3. Usser ad Seldenum, Epist. 51.

What emotions must have filled his heart! By that rock he once had his Bethel. By that brook he had wrestled with God, and had his Peniel. Under yonder oak he had songs and visions of the night. Below him stood the house of his former master, who had used him so roughly twenty-three years before. What a joyful mission to enter those doors and tell the glad tidings of a Saviour! But, lo! that house is seen to be in flames, if we may credit the legend. The tyrant has heard of Patrick's coming. He is troubled. An evil spirit possesses him. He determines not to meet the missionary. He sets fire to the house, and casts himself into the flames, choosing to perish rather than to become the disciple of his former slave. Patrick sees it, and for three hours weeps in compassion. But he next is represented as uttering his curse upon the family of the suicide, and declaring that none of Milchu's sons shall ever sit upon his pretty throne; they shall be slaves for ever!

Thus had Patrick cursed the rivers that would yield him no fish, according to the fables of the monks. "Let us hope," says Dr. Todd, "that these examples of vengeance, so common in his story, represent only the mind of the ecclesiastics of a later age, and that his biographers knew not the spirit he was of."*

If there be any truth at all in the account of the visit to his former master, it is probable that Patrick failed in his efforts. He could not convince the tyrant that Christ was a Saviour. Baffled and repelled, he left him in his sins. Those sins were the flames into which he cast himself. But the monks could not bear to have their hero defeated, and they portrayed the self-destruction of his former master. One account is that some of the cruel prince's family were afterward converted to the faith.

Again we find the missionary at Sabhal, in what is now the barony of Secale. There he preaches for many days, going about in the neigbourhood, teaching all who will give heed to his words. "The faith began to spread." It was not by outward display that the hearts of the people were gained; not by exhibiting relics, not by holding up a crucifix with an image upon it, nor by the mumbling of a Latin mass; but by the preaching of God's holy word in the language of the natives. He had learned their speech while a slave, if indeed it had not been to him as a mother tongue.

* Todd's St. Patrick, p. 406.

He may have called them around him at the beat of a drum, and he pointed them to the true cross of Calvary. Having formed little bands of disciples and placed teachers over them, he planned other missionary journeys.

It seems to have been Patrick's policy to bring the rulers of the land first to the faith. Eleven centuries after him the Reformers acted somewhat upon this principle: Luther sought to gain the Saxon princes; Calvin presented to Francis I. one of the noblest letters ever written, and before other kings he laid his simple Confession of Faith. The Irish chieftains and kings had great power over their tribes in the fifth century. The men of influence were gathered at their courts. To win them was a great point, for "kings might become nursing-fathers, and queens nursing-mothers" to the infant Church.

Tarah was before the mind of Saint Patrick. Thither he must go and there preach Christ. It was the chief centre of power. There were gathered the kings, princes, nobles and warriors. There were held the national conventions every three years. The supreme monarch of Ireland was Laogaire, who had reigned but three or four years before the coming of Patrick. He was about to summon the great convention to meet him at Tarah. It was the parliament of that ancient day, according to an old Irish poet:

> "The learned Ollam Fodla first ordained
> The great assembly, where the nobles met,
> And priests, and poets, and philosophers,
> To make new laws, and to correct the old,
> And to advance the honour of his country."

Patrick resolved to attend this convention. Taking his boat, he and his companions sailed down the coast and entered the mouth of the river Boyne. Thence they took their way on foot toward the place where now stands the town of Slane. Coming one evening to the house of a nobleman named Sechnen, they were received with generous hospitality. The guests sang, prayed, read the Scriptures and spake of the errand on which Jesus Christ came into the world. The host let the truth sink down into his ears and reach his heart. He believed and was baptized. It was very common in those days for missionaries to baptize persons within a few hours of their conversion. Thus did the apostles, but in their case the believers generally had some knowledge of the Scriptures beforehand, as in the case of the believers at Pentecost, the Ethiopian officer, and probably the centurion at Cæsarea. This custom, however, in later days led to baptism upon a very slight evidence of true faith. It often secured only a nominal Christianity.

In this family of rank was a young man of gentle nature, attractive and impressible. The looks and words of the chief stranger won his heart; Patrick also was charmed with him. He determined to be a disciple and follow the missionary wherever he went. His parents and friends tried to divert him from such a purpose. They set forth the dangers and the toils of such a life as he must have before him. But none of these things moved him. He left his home to be a missionary— the first, it seems, of the natives who was reared for the ministry. He could not be separated from Patrick, keeping close to him for years amid all his dangers and sufferings. We know not his native name, but for his gentleness he was called Benignus, or Binen. God had given him the power of song, and he used it for good. He sang the praises of the Lord before large assemblies, to whom Patrick preached. Thus he rendered great aid to the good cause. He was the Asaph of the movement.

Patrick hastened onward, and pitched his tent

on a hill quite near to Tarah. It may have been the time of Easter, and he may have kept it according to the general custom of the fifth century. The practice of setting apart certain days for worship, in memory of great events in the life of our Lord, grew up quite early in the Church. It sprang from a good intention. But it soon became a form and a device of men. Instead of keeping every Sabbath in memory of Christ's resurrection, they observed one day in the year, and called it Easter. No such custom is taught in the New Testament. The "holy day" has become a holiday with most of those who pay any regard to it. In the time of Patrick it was held more sacred. It became a stirring question in the Irish Church on what day it should be kept. The Latin Christians held to one day, and the Greek Christians another. We have little doubt that Patrick kept Easter in the Greek manner (if he kept it at all), for thus did the Irish Church in later centuries. But we are far from being sure that he went to Tarah at Easter-tide, and that his "paschal fire" on the hill drew the attention of the king and threw the whole court into commotion.

Romish biographers make this a strong point for their dates in the life of St. Patrick. They assume that the Feast of Tarah was celebrated at the vernal equinox. In 433 this occurred on the 26th of March. This they take as the Easter of that year. They also assume that Patrick kept his first Easter in Ireland that very year. According to their story he must have done a great deal of sailing, foot-travelling and open-air preaching during the winter months. But the year 441 would better agree with their own argument, drawn from the movements of the sun. Also it seems that the feast of Tarah came off in May, for Beltine's day is still fixed at that time among the Irish and the Scottish Highlanders. Some ancient authorities, however, fix the convention of Tarah about the first of November, a time still further from the Christian Easter. Moreover, there is some evidence that Saint Patrick was not at Tarah for several years after his arrival in Ireland.* Indeed we should not be guilty of very great incredulity if we doubted whether he was ever there at all when such a convention was held. The proof, to say the least of it, is by no means conclusive.

There was a vast work before the missionary. A heathen religion must be overthrown, one of the most powerful and interesting of the ancient

* Todd's St. Patrick, pp. 412–420.

systems of errors. We must therefore give a little attention to the Druids, their customs, their superstitions, their poets, their priests and their influence over both rulers and people.

CHAPTER VIII.

THE DRUIDS.

> Through untold ages past there stood
> A deep, wild, sacred, awful wood:
> Its interwoven boughs had made
> A cheerless, chilly, silent shade:
> There, underneath the gloomy trees,
> Were oft performed the mysteries
> Of barbarous priests, who thought that God
> Loved to look down upon the sod
> Where every leaf was deeply stained
> With blood from human victims drained.
> LUCAN, iii. 399.

UPON the larger branches of old oaks grew the mistletoe. It was a shrub fixing its roots into the wood of the tree, and there it appeared dark and green through all the winter, with white berries upon it. It is often seen in forests along our Western rivers. I have seen one specimen upon a white oak as far to the north as the southern shores of Lake Michigan. The mistletoe was held sacred by the heathens of Northern Europe. The shade of the oak on which it grew was their place of worship. Hence, probably, the name Druids, or the men of the oaks.

We imagine ourselves in Ireland, far back, fourteen centuries ago. We stand upon a hill with a village in front of us, just on the border of a thick, wild forest. It is one of the first evenings in May. Out of some cabins and cells we see strange-looking men creeping. They walk about very solemnly, and whisper something which to us is very mysterious. They are venerable long-beards and magicians. Some of them wear coats of many colours, and a string of serpent's eggs about their necks. Others have a white scarf thrown over their shoulders, bracelets on their arms and long white rods in their hands. They gaze at the stars, and decide that it is the proper time for their sacred rites. The moon is just six days old. They gather about their chief, but we prefer not to be in their crowd.

In solemn procession they march into the dark, gloomy woods. Under an ancient oak they halt and engage in a strange mummery. One of their priests climbs the oak, and with the golden knife cuts away the wondrous mistletoe. Carefully he throws it down upon a white cloth, and they quite adore it. Every leaf is a treasure. They think it has power to charm away evil spirits and keep them in health.

But this is not all. They have led with them two white bullocks for sacrifice. They now put a wreath of oak leaves upon their horns, and prepare for solemn rites. The golden knife is plunged into the necks of these victims, which fall quivering in the pangs of death. The fires are kindled. Skilful hands make all the arrangements for a feast.* We will not suppose ourselves to be gazing upon a more horrid sight, for the Druids are represented as leading into the gloomy woods some slave, or prisoner of war, or the child of some peasant, and there offering a human sacrifice. At such times the singing priests are said to have roared and howled and beat their drums to drown the cries of the suffering martyrs. Cæsar tells us that the Druids of Gaul made huge baskets of osier, in the shape of a man, filled them with human beings, and set the vast mass on fire.† Let us hope that the ancient Irish were not so barbarous.

Such worship reminds us of the horrid rites of sacrifice to Baal and Moloch. It has been sup-

---

* Pliny, lib. xvi. cap. 44.
† Commentaries, lib. vi. 16.

posed that Druidism came from the Phœnicians, from whom the Hebrews derived their worst forms of idolatry. The Druids had their Baal, as appears from their Beltine* fires. To face the sun was to be about right in the world. The word *south* meant *right*, and *north* meant *wrong*. If one was beginning any work, he must first look toward the sun if he would prosper. A boat going to sea must turn sunwise. As soon as people were married they must make a turn sunwise. The dead were borne sunwise to the grave. Perhaps this was one reason why Dichu wished the new church to face the south. The fronting of buildings toward the east may have had a similar meaning. Certain men, who think that they must turn toward sunrise when saying their prayers, may ask whether they do not take their custom from the Druids, whose priests were likely to do the same thing. Thus follies creep into the very Church of Christ. They perhaps adored the sun, but they do not seem to have made idols. They held that their gods were omnipresent, and to be worshipped in roofless temples or within large circles of stones. Some writers have thought that

* Beal-tain, Beal's fire-day. Beal means the sun; in honour of the sun the fire was made.

they had their chief seats in Ireland and on the Isle of Man; thence they spread over Britain and into Gaul.

Saint Patrick might lay hold of some of their doctrines, and thus gain a footing for his own. They were ready to listen when he told them that God was everywhere, always having his eye upon their deeds. They believed in the immortality of the soul, and had some crude ideas of future rewards and punishments. They taught that there was another world, where the good souls preserved their identity and their habits. The souls of bad men, they thought, passed into lower animals to be chastised. At funerals letters were burnt, for the dead to read or carry to those who had gone before them across the borders of the spirit-land. Money was also loaned to the departed, on condition that it should be repaid in the world to come.* The priests were careful to be the bankers, quite as certain priests now are, who receive money to purchase souls out of purgatory. But what a work to clear a few truths from a mass of errors! The missionary must preach Christ, who offered the only redeeming sacrifice, and brought life and immortality to light in the gospel. He must declare

* Michelet, Hist. France, i. chap. 2.

the facts of a judgment, a hell, a heaven, and an eternity. Druidism was to the ancient Irish what Brahminism now is to the Asiatics; the work of Patrick was quite similar to that of the modern missionary among the Hindoos.

In going to Tarah, the citadel of Druidism, Patrick must meet the priests and bards of a false religion. These men had great influence at the royal court, and to this day it remains in Ireland, as "Kirwan" has shown us:

"The power of these priests was very great. They directed in all sacred things—they offered all sacrifices—they were the teachers of the youth, and the judges in all disputes public and private. Their supreme pontiff was elected by these priests in conclave assembled; and he was called the *Archdruid*, and possessed power without check or control. Whilst thus the ministers of the law, they enforced their decisions by religious sanctions, and if any refused obedience to their decrees they forbid their presence at all religious sacrifices. The persons thus doomed were regarded as accursed, and were shunned as were those white with leprosy by the Jews.

"These priests were exempt from war and from taxation, and were regarded with the deepest veneration. Their learning was not committed to writing, lest it should go down among the people; it was committed to memory, and was thus transmitted from one to another. When they committed anything to writing, it is said they used the Greek language, of which the people were utterly ignorant.

"Many of the customs and superstitions which now exist in Ireland, and which are wielded with great power by the priests to gain their purposes, existed there long before the days of Saint Patrick. The peasantry now bury their dead with peculiar rites; they have their wakes, when the neighbours watch with the dead and carouse; lighted candles are placed around the corpse; the dead are taken to the grave followed by the wailing multitudes, and are buried with their feet toward the east. So it was two thousand years ago; thus Dathy, the last pagan prince of the country, was buried.

"They have now their *holy wells* in Ireland. They exist in great numbers in every part of the country; and all have a history which connects them with the fantastic doings of some saint or saintess in remote antiquity. It is truly painful to see the deep paths worn by pilgrims to them, going round and round them on their knees, doing penance for their sins. At the canonical time for visiting these wells the paths around them are red with the blood of the poor pilgrims. Around these wells are rude stones, among which the poor people stuff some of their rags, and even some of their hair, as a witness, if necessary, of their visit; and around these wells are holy bushes, on which are always streaming some fragments of pilgrim garments to put the guardian saint of the well in mind of 'the stations' there performed. As to these wells there can be no doubt; I have visited them recently, and have seen the things now described. The name of Saint Patrick, and of a Saint Bridget, are widely associated with these fountains; but they were regarded as holy before the Christian era; and the penances now performed around them, and in the same manner and form, were performed in obedience to Druid priests two thousand years ago. Indeed, Thomas Moore, himself a papist, admits that the holy St. Bridget, of whom Alban Butler so piously writes, was the Vesta of the fire-worshippers; and that the nuns of St. Bridget were only the Druidesses continued under a new name!

"Who, born in Ireland, or descended from Irish parents, has not heard of fairies, and of their doings and antics, until he has feared if not believed their existence? There is scarcely any form of superstition which has more generally seized on the Irish mind than this. The shoe of an ass is often nailed on the door-sill to keep off the fairies. The priests bless amulets, which are sold for 'a compensation,' and are worn around the neck, to keep off the witches and the fairies! When a boy or girl sent to a Protestant school gets sick, the priest, even in our own day, tells the parents that their child is bewitched in punishment for going to those awful schools, and offers to drive off the witches for 'a compensation,' and on the condition that the child be withdrawn from the schools. If the child gets well, the priest has the credit; if it dies, the parents and child have gone too far to have the punishment remitted! But these fairy legends and superstitions are of Druid origin, and have been adopted and transmitted by the priests to work upon the fears of the people.

"There are bushes sacred to the fairies, and 'pleasant hills' where they love to congregate, and lonely towers amid whose ruins they love to gambol by moonlight, and groves sacred to their sports and meetings. To cut down a fairy bush is even now a sacrilege among the ignorant. And the instances are not, even in our day, unfrequent of a peasant removing his cabin when ignorantly built on the pathway of the fairies, or when found in their way when opening up a new path. All, again of Druidic origin, whose priests had their fairies, and their bushes, their hills, groves and places sacred to them!

"The Irish peasantry have a remarkable fondness for bonfires. On Saint John's Eve they kindle them on the hill-tops all over the country. The lovely Charlotte Elizabeth thus describes one of these of which she was a witness: The pile, composed of turf, bog-wood and other combustibles, was built to a great height. 'Early in the evening the peasants began to assemble, all habited in their best array, glowing with health; I had never seen anything resembling it; and was exceedingly delighted with their handsome, intelligent, merry faces. The fire being kindled, a splendid blaze shot up. After a pause the ground was cleared in the front of an old piper, the very beau-ideal of drollery and shrewdness, who, seated in a low chair, with a well-replenished jug by his side, screwed his pipes to the liveliest tunes, and the endless jig began.

"'When the fire burned low, an indispensable part of the ceremony commenced. Every one present of the peasantry passed through it, and several children were thrown across the sparkling embers.' And after describing other ludicrous scenes, she remarks, 'Here was the old pagan worship of Baal, if not of Moloch too, carried on openly and universally in the heart of a nominally Christian country, and by millions professing the Christian name. I was confounded, for I did not know, then, that Popery is only a crafty adaptation of pagan idolatries to its own scheme.'

"The Druids were fire-worshippers, as were the Asiatics from whom they were descended. The priests of Rome adopted the days and the customs consecrated to the worship of fire; they called the days after a saint, and gave to the ceremonies a papal significance; and thus perpetuated the ceremonies of the Druids to our time.

"The kings had their bards, as had also all the great aristocratic families. These bards became, in time, a privileged class, and exercised great influence. They were the chief chroniclers; they kept the family genealogies; they cast into rude verse the deeds of their heroes, and, like Homer in Greece, recited them on public occasions. On great occasions, and at all great festivals, these bards were present. By their example they excited the youth to the cultivation of oratory, and by their fervid appeals they swayed the multitude, and filled them with the highest enthusiasm. They moved the people as the high winds move the trees of the forest. They would seize their harps and play and sing their own national songs, in which the people would join, until the family, provincial, or national spirit was intensely excited, when all were ready to go forth to deeds of heroism or of rapine. And the names of some of these bards, or Fileas, are retained and honoured among the people of the country to the present day. Had the productions of these bards escaped the wrecks of time, Ireland, too, might have its Homer, its Virgil, its Horace and its Ossian!

"There are long and dreary annals running through ages, which record little else than the rise and fall of kings—the wars between provinces and petty nobles—the insurrections of the peasants against their oppressors—and the way in which nobles at the head of their retainers ravaged the island, and destroyed everything by fire and sword. By causes like these, and by the bloody rites and superstitions of the Druids, the people were wasted and brutalized. The arts introduced by the first colonists were neglected—agriculture was forsaken; and, save at intervals few and far between, the entire island was agitated by the jealousies and conflicts of contending princes and nobles, until in the process of time the people were buried in profound barbarism and ignorance.

"Through those obscure ages rose various customs, traces of which are now visible. . The people were divided in ranks and grades. These grades were designated by the number of colours they were permitted to wear; the lowest could wear but one, and none but the royal family could wear seven. The rank next to royalty was composed of the learned order; these wore six colours, which shows the high estimation of learning in that early day. This custom is the origin of the Scotch plaid worn by the Highlanders down to our own times.

The Irish are proverbial for their hospitality. In those early times provisions were made by law for strangers and travellers, by creating an order of nobility called *entertainers*. These dignitaries were required to be the proprietors of seven townlands; to have seven ploughs at work; to have seven herds of cows, each herd to contain one hundred and forty; their mansion was required to be accessible by four different avenues; and a hog, sheep and beef were required to be in constant preparation, that whoever called should be fed without delay. And all was gratuitous. Thus the hospitality of the Milesians was without a parallel in Europe; and such is the character of the Irish people to the present time. The houses of the Irish gentry are now as open as they were under the law promulged from the old halls of Tarah; and in the poorest mud cottage on the side of the moor you will receive a kind welcome, and, if you are in want, a warmth of sympathy that will divide with you the last cup of porridge or the last potato. 'An Irish welcome' is proverbial in all the earth for cheerfulness, heartiness and truthfulness. And the Milesians have carried with them into all the lands of their dispersion this characteristic of their ancestry. May they never lose it!

"These are national characteristics which have their foundation in institutions older than our Christianity; and which, because of the *stationary principle* which has obtained in Ireland, have been transmitted to our time. Once break, as it must be broken in our country, the influence of that old stationary principle; save the native impulses of the Milesians, but elevate them above the influence

SAINT PATRICK. 137

of the social and Druidical laws of old Ollamh Fodhla, and the conventions of Tarah,—and you have material out of which to form as noble a people as walk the earth."*

If Druidism thus stamped itself upon a people, so that its customs were not all removed by Christianity, what must it have been when Saint Patrick began his labours in Ireland? Its priests and poets were the learned men of the country. Twenty years of study were required to educate a Druid. He knew something of the sciences of mathematics, astronomy, rhetoric, law, medicine and moral philosophy. He was skilled in the arts of magic. His knowledge was condensed into triads, or sentences each containing three strong points. One triad ran thus: " The first three principles of wisdom are—obedience to the laws of God, care for the welfare of man and fortitude under the accidents of life."

Woe to Saint Patrick if a Druid grew jealous! A single word from a Druid for ever withered a human being; he was "cut down like grass." He always had the king's ear, and at his whisper the cruel order went forth to slay the hated man. On

* Ireland and the Irish, by Kirwan (Rev. N. Murray, D. D.), N. Y. Observer, 1855.

his lip was war or peace; in his hand the golden knife for the throat of the condemned; at the sound of his rude lyre the people rose to the work of vengeance; on his word the doom of a kingdom hung. The loyalty of the land was a religion of wonder and fear, and to dispute with a Druid was a crime against the state.*

Woe also to the disciples of Saint Patrick if they kept back the tax claimed by the Druids! The chief Druid of every district required all families, rich or poor, to pay him certain annual dues. On an evening in autumn they must put out every fire in their houses. It seems to have been at the time of the convention of Tarah. Then every man must appear and pay his tax. If he failed, he was the object of terrible vengeance. To be with a fire in the house, and without money in the hand, was a crime. The next morning the Druid priest allowed every man to take some of his own sacred fire, and rekindle the flame on his own hearth. It was a crime for one man to lend a living coal to his neighbour; if he did it, he was reduced to poverty and declared an outlaw.† To be a Christian one must renounce

---

* Disraeli, Amenities, i. 1.
† Toland's His. Druids, pp. 71. 72.

such customs of superstition at the peril of his life. Also, if he saw "the fiery cross" borne on the hills, he must rush to the rallying-place of the clans. The chieftain had slain a goat, dipped in its blood the ends of a wooden cross, set it on fire, given it to the clansman, and told him to run and wave it on the hill-tops. When his breath was gone, another would take it up and repeat the signal. The man who did not obey the summons was doomed.

CHAPTER IX.

SAINT PATRICK'S ARMOUR.

THE story is that King Laogaire and his court were preparing for the great feast held at the time of the convention at Tarah. One of the oldest writers upon Saint Patrick, in his fondness for the Scripture style, says: "Now there happened in that year the idolatrous festival which the Gentiles were wont to observe with many incantations and magical inventions, and some other superstitions of idolatry; gathering together the kings, satraps, dukes, chieftains and nobles of the people; summoning the magicians, enchanters, augurs, with the inventors or teachers of every art and gift, unto Laogaire (as unto King Nebuchadnezzar of old) to Tarah, which was their Babylon. . . . They were worshipping and exercising themselves in that Gentile festivity." *

Every fire was to be put out in the land, and it was "made known by proclamation to all that

* Muirchu Maccu-Machtene, an Irish writer supposed to be of the seventh century.—*Vide Todd's Saint Patrick*, chap. iii.

whosoever should, on that night, kindle a fire before the king's fire had been kindled on the hill of Tarah, that soul should be cut off from his people." We may imagine that

> "The king was seated on a royal throne,
> And in his face majestic greatness shone:
> A monarch for heroic deeds designed,
> For noble acts become a noble mind:
> About him, summoned by his strict command,
> The peers, the priests and commons of the land,
> In princely state and solemn order stand."

The night is falling. Not yet have the Druids struck their sacred fire on the hill of Tarah. Death to the man who dares to kindle his own in the very teeth of the law! The king looks out of his window; the glare of a distant flame catches his eye. He is amazed. Is his sovereignty despised? "Who is this that sets at naught the law?" he inquires. "Who is so defiant as to light his fire just in sight of my palace?"

"Death to him!" mutter the Druid counsellors, who are in still greater alarm. All eyes stand out with astonishment. The word runs though the halls, "There is a fire on yonder hill."

"What shall be done?" asks the king, who is scarcely permitted to have a mind of his own. It is a religious offence; the priests must give their advice.

"O king, live for ever!" is the reply of the Druids, as framed by our old author, who labours to imitate the style of Scripture and make the scene parallel to events in Daniel's time. "This fire which we see shall never be extinguished to all eternity unless we put it out to-night. Moreover, it shall prevail over all the fires of our wonted observance; and he who has kindled it shall prevail over us and over thyself, and shall win away from thee all the men of thy kingdom." Well had it been for the Druids if they had known Scripture so familiarly as to play thus upon the words of Daniel to the king in Babylon! They would not have been in such alarm.

"Now," continues our author, "when King Laogaire heard all these things he was greatly troubled, as Herod was of old, and all the city of Tarah with him. And he answered and said, 'This shall not be so, but we will now go and see the end of the matter, and we will take and kill the men who are doing such wickedness against our kingdom.'"

The story is, that the king set out for the fire-crowned hill, with numerous courtiers in his train.

The Druids would not permit the king nor any of the valiant knights to venture too close, lest some strange power should injure them. Coming to a halt, they advised that the daring intruder should be brought into the royal presence. "Let none rise up at his coming," said they, "nor pay him any respect, lest he win them by his arts."

The man was ordered to appear. He at once obeyed. He entered among the horses and chariots and the array of courtiers, chanting the words, "Some trust in chariots and some in horses, but we will remember the name of the Lord our God."

All eyes were upon the dignified and courageous stranger. One of the royal attendants rose up from respect to him. This was Erc Mac Dego, a noble young man, to whom the stranger said, "Why do you alone rise up to me in honour of my God."

"I know not why," was the answer; "it seems as if fire comes from your lips to mine."

"Wilt thou receive the baptism of the Lord?"

"I will receive it when I know who thou art."

"I am Patrick, a messenger of Christ to all who will hear the truth of heaven." We are not bound to believe all this, even after having culled a few reasonable statements from a mass of absurdities. But there is added in the legends an account of wonders performed by Patrick, modelled after the miracles wrought by the hand of Moses before Pharaoh, except that Moses is utterly outdone. Very coolly does Father Brenan say: "The conference which on this occasion took place between Saint Patrick and Laogaire is so interwoven with unattested and incredible anecdote that it might perhaps be as well passed over.* We pass it over.

The king is furious. He orders his people to seize Patrick. But the fearless missionary chants the words, "Let God arise, and let his enemies be scattered." We may suppose that he explained the matter of his fire on the hill. It had nothing to do with Easter, and, even if it had, the royal pagan would have cared nothing for that. It was kindled before his tent, simply to expel the chill of an October night. The king is appeased. Irish wrath quickly gives way to a generous Irish forgiveness. As the missionary is a stranger, he shall receive Irish hospitality from some of the nobles.

The next day, Patrick, with five of his companions, enters the hall where the court is feasting. The king's chief bard rises to greet him. This is Dubtach, a Druid of great learning and fame. With him also rises the young poet Fiacc, a stu-

* Eccl. Hist. Ireland, p. 14.

dent whom he taught in the Druid lore. They listen while the missionary preaches what they never heard before. He is represented as saying to the king and the magnates of the convention: "You worship the sun; you adore the light; it is but a mere creature. That sun which you see rises daily for our good at the command of the Almighty, but its splendour shall not always endure. The day will come when its light shall be extinguished, and all those that worship it shall miserably perish. But we adore the true Sun, Christ the Lord and Ruler of all the world." The poet-laureate and his young disciple saw the folly of the fire-worship, the leading doctrine of Irish Druidism. They renounced the system. They believed the word and were the first converts at Tarah. The younger of these two poets might have found a genial friend in Benignus, the sweet singer of the Irish Israel. The king was touched by the prayer of Patrick. Troubled, fearing, trembling and seeking relief, he said to his counsellors: "It is better for me to believe than to die." He professed himself a believer in Christ. But it would take a large mantle of charity to cover his sins. He seems to have acted from policy, rather than principle. The account is, that many at Tarah believed, and that "Patrick baptized many thousand men on that day." No doubt this is an exaggeration.

We may know much of Saint Patrick's spirit amid these scenes if we may give credit to an ancient Irish hymn as one written by himself. It is often called Saint Patrick's Armour. It is in the style of a *lorica* or prayer against all evil powers. Some parts of it are still remembered by the Irish peasantry, and repeated at bed-time as a protection from evil. Thus words of devotion have been turned to a sort of superstitious dream. "That this hymn is a composition of great antiquity cannot be questioned. It is written in a very ancient dialect of the Irish Celtic. . . . It notices no doctrine or practice of the Church that is not known to have existed before the fifth century. . . . We may not, therefore, err very much in taking this hymn as a fair representation of Saint Patrick's faith and teaching. Whether it was actually written by him or not, it was certainly composed at a period not very far distant from his times, with a view to represent and put forth his sentiments. . . . Notwithstanding some tincture of superstition, we find the pure and undoubted truths of Christianity, a firm faith in the protecting providence and power of God; and Christ is made

SAINT PATRICK. 147

all and in all.* None of the peculiar errors of the Rome of the eighth century are found in it. Were it "a pious fraud" of the monks, it would certainly have had praises to the Virgin Mary, appeals to angels and saints, and hints concerning the power of relics, charms and rosaries. It is thus literally rendered by Dr. Todd:

> I. I bind to myself† to-day
> The strong power of the invocation of the Trinity,
> The faith of the Trinity in Unity,
> The Creator of the elements.
>
> II. I bind to myself to-day
> The power of the incarnation of Christ,
> With that of his baptism;
> The power of the crucifixion,
> With that of his burial;
> The power of the resurrection,
> With [that of] the ascension;
> The power of the coming
> To the sentence of judgment.
>
> III. I bind to myself to-day
> The power of the love of seraphim,
> In the obedience of angels,
> In the hope of resurrection unto reward,

---

* Todd's St. Patrick, pp. 425-432.

† Dr. Todd shows that this is the true rendering of the word *Atomriug*, usually translated "At Tarah." This lessens the evidence that the hymn was first used at this royal seat.

In the prayers of the noble fathers,
In the predictions of the prophets,
In the preaching of apostles,
In the faith of confessors,
In the purity of holy virgins,
In the acts of righteous men.

IV. I bind to myself to-day
    The power of heaven,
    The light of the sun,
    The whiteness of snow,
    The force of fire,
    The flashing of lightning,
    The velocity of wind,
    The depth of the sea,
    The stability of the earth,
    The hardness of rocks.

V. I bind to myself to-day
    The power of God to guide me,
    The might of God to uphold me,
    The wisdom of God to teach me,
    The eye of God to watch over me,
    The ear of God to hear me,
    The word of God to give me speech,
    The hand of God to protect me,
    The way of God to prevent me,
    The shield of God to shelter me,
    The host of God to defend me,

        Against the snares of demons,
        Against the temptations of vices,

Against the lusts of nature,
Against every man who meditates injury to me,
Whether far or near,
With few or with many.

VI. I have set around me all these powers,
Against every hostile, savage power
Directed against my body and my soul;
Against the incantations of false prophets,
Against the black laws of heathenism,
Against the false laws of heresy,
Against the deceits of idolatry,
Against the spells of women, and smiths, and Druids,
Against all knowledge which blinds the soul of man.

VII. Christ, protect me to-day
Against poison, against burning,
Against drowning, against wound,
That I may receive abundant reward.

VIII. Christ with me, Christ before me,
Christ behind me, Christ within me,
Christ beneath me, Christ above me,
Christ at my right, Christ at my left,
Christ in the fort [when I am at home],
Christ in the chariot-seat [when I travel],
Christ in the ship [when I sail].

IX. Christ in the heart of every man
Who thinks of me;
Christ in the mouth of every man
Who speaks to me;

Christ in every eye that sees me,
Christ in every ear that hears me.

X. Of the Lord is salvation,
Christ is salvation,
With us ever be
Thy salvation, O Lord.

CHAPTER X.

CAUSES OF SUCCESS.

IT is not our intention to relate all the travels and heroic adventures attributed to Saint Patrick by those biographers who have dealt largely in the wonderful and miraculous. They rarely ascribed to him a failure; almost every prince whom he visits is suddenly converted; wherever he goes whole districts are won to the faith, and a bishop is placed over the group of churches. This looks suspicious on its very face. The greatest missionaries, from the Apostle Paul downward, have had defeats. Uniform success has rarely been the rule in human toils. The wise advantage taken of a defeat is quite as much to the honour of a hero as an unbroken series of victories.

No doubt there was some romance in his preaching, and on his journeys various strange exploits. But the tendency has been to exaggerate his labours. "Many of those adventures were evidently invented to pay a compliment to certain tribes, or clans, by ascribing the conversion of their ancestors to the preaching of Saint Patrick. Others were intended to claim for certain churches, or monasteries, the honour of having been by him founded: and others, again, were framed with the object of supporting the pretensions of the see of Armagh to the possession of lands or jurisdiction in various parts of Ireland."* Very singular is it, if he made so many dioceses, that one modern author names twenty† of them as founded before the close of the fifth century. Of this statement we shall find hereafter an explanation. They were central, missionary churches, each having a bishop in the sense of a pastor over his own flock, and the general oversight of the little bands of Christians in his district.

What were the causes of Patrick's success? On this question we may hang what is farther to be related. We shall take those statements which seem most likely to be true, illustrating them with such anecdotes as exhibit the character of the man and of his religious teachings.

A commanding presence seems to have lent its aid. Tradition portrays him as attractive, venera-

* Todd's St. Patrick, 400.
† Brenan, Eccl. Hist. Ireland, chap. ii.

ble and dignified in his appearance. In his looks there was a majesty of love and truth. A portly frame, open countenance and imposing manner are not essential elements of usefulness. The Apostle Paul was "in bodily presence contemptible," but he was a preacher of tremendous power. The ardent piety shining forth through uncomely features is often a means of grace. Yet among an ignorant, superstitious, barbarous people there is a force in a noble presence. Chieftains appear to have seen something in Patrick more stately than was in themselves.

He went from Tarah to the Tailten races. The court resorted thither to engage in the royal diversions. A modern Irish fair would be a more promising scene for preaching. But in spite of the tilts, tournaments and rough sports of the Irish Olympia, he gained the heart of large numbers of people. He bade fair to turn the amusements into solemn exercises. The Druid of longest, grayest beard could not thus sway the multitude. Numbers listened and believed, according to the traditions. But the king's brother, Carbri, son of the great Niall of the Nine Hostages, grew angry when he feared that the games would be spoiled. It is likely that a Druid whispered revenge in his ear.

He first sought to kill the missionary, but his brother Conall warded off the blow. He then caused Patrick's helpers to be beaten and thrown into the Blackwater. They were not drowned. Persecution won them sympathy.

Conall opened the doors of his heart and home to the preacher, inquired the way of life, believed on the Lord, and with great joy was baptized; thus accepting brotherhood with the lowliest peasant who had bound himself to Christ. Months of preaching were passed in this region. "Show kindness to my believing children," said the missionary, "and be just all the days of your life."

"I devote to the Lord," said the prince, "the site for a church." He measured the ground with his own feet, and ordered that it should be sixty foot-lengths long. There stood the building which took the name of "the Great Church of Patrick." This Conall was the great-grandfather of Columba, the renowned missionary at Iona and in Western Scotland.

His mode of teaching is worthy of note. It was direct, full of truth and forcible. It related to Christ rather than to the Church. A very curious and ancient anecdote, whether true or false, affords a specimen of what was believed to be his manner of instructing the ignorant. He crossed the Shannon and went into Connaught, and lingered near the Mount of the Druids in Roscommon. Perhaps he mused upon the fact that races perish from the earth as well as men, as he passed by the cemetery of the ancient kings. Perhaps he found hospitality in the royal fort. Near it was a well-known fountain. Thither he and his companions went one morning, it would seem, to talk with those who came for water. The little company was afterward magnified into "a synod of holy bishops!" It is said that there they lifted their early song of praise to God.

It appears that King Laogaire had sent two of his daughters into this neighbourhood, and placed them under the care of two Druids. For a morning walk they came to the fountain, and were much surprised to meet the strangers, not being quite sure but they were "men of the hills," or half gods, who were supposed to dwell in the mountain caves.

"Whence are ye?" they asked, "and whence come ye?"

"It were better for you to confess to our true God than to inquire concerning our race."

"Who is God, and where does he dwell?" the

elder asked. "Has he sons and daughters, silver and gold? Is he ever-living? Does he love his children? Are they beautiful? Tell us of him. How shall he be seen? Is it in youth or in old age that he is to be found?"

"Our God is the God of all men," answered Patrick. "He is the God of heaven and earth, the sea and the rivers, the mountains and the valleys, the sun, the moon and the stars. He is in heaven, and above heaven. He dwells also on the earth. He gives life to all things—light to the sun, stars to the sky, water to the fountains, and he upholds all beings."

How different was he from the gods of the Druids! If we had never heard of the true God, we might understand how the king's daughters wondered. But they were to hear a still greater truth—one which had power to win the heart of all who will give due heed to it. Those, who call it a mystery and treat it with neglect, know not how precious it is to the sinner seeking the way to be saved.

"He hath a Son co-eternal and co-equal with himself," continued Patrick. "The Son is not younger than the Father; nor the Father older than the Son. And the Holy Ghost breatheth in them.* The Father, the Son and the Holy Ghost are not divided. But I wish to unite you to the heavenly King, as ye are the daughters of an earthly king; that is, to believe."

"Teach us most diligently how we may believe in the heavenly King. Show us how we may see him face to face, and whatsoever thou wilt say unto us we will do?"

No doubt here is a blank in the lesson. If the scene were real, the plain requirements must have been taught. And Patrick said: "Believe ye that by baptism ye put off the sin of your father and your mother?"†

"We believe."

"Believe ye in repentance after sin?"

"We believe."

"Believe ye in the unity of the Church?"

"We believe."

Nothing more is added that illustrates Patrick's method of teaching. In this there is not all that

* "Inflat in eis," proceedeth from them, would have been the truth.

† The error here may have been that of the biographer, rather than of Patrick. Original sin is not put away by baptism; its removal by Christ may be indicated. The sign must not be taken for the cause. This error grew up quite early in some parts of the Christian Church.

we could wish. There are some errors. But there is nothing here of modern Romanism. On their confession of faith the king's daughters were baptized at the same fountain. What is said of their wish to "see the face of Christ" and their sudden death is evidently the boldest fiction.

The story also is, that their teachers were converted "to the repentance of God." They believed and renounced their Druidism. Near this spot a church arose. That many Druids were converted is very credible. If only a few of them had accepted the Christian doctrines, we should expect to find more persecution and less success.

His power of adaptation must have aided Patrick's influence. There is a beautiful story which gives nobility to one of the plainest of plants. It is said that Patrick once came to a barbarous tribe and began to preach to them in the open air. He spoke of the Holy Trinity. They shook their heads. It was too sublime a mystery for an ignorant and faithless people, who would not accept as true what they could not comprehend. These rationalists grew indignant and intolerant. They were about to enter into the controversy with clubs and drive the missionary from their soil. He understood the wise management of human nature.

Stooping down, he took from the green sod a sprig which had three leaves united in one, and holding it up he gave a simple illustration of the Trinity. It was the common shamrock, trodden under foot in the pastures and the wild woods. The ears of the people were gained, quite as much by the tact of the strange preacher as by the force of the argument drawn from a symbol so imperfect and unworthy of the theme. They listened to the proofs of the doctrine given in the Scriptures, and were convinced. The legend is that the shamrock became in this way a national emblem of Ireland. In our times many an Irish hat is decked with the shamrock on Saint Patrick's day.

His treatment of superstition aided Patrick's influence. It appears that he overthrew some of the pillar-stones, which seem to have been the chief objects of worship with the pagan Irish. One of these was the *Crom-cruach*, or "the black stooping-stone." Keating says it was "the same god that Zoroaster adored in Greece," and that this was the first form of idolatry introduced among "the Milesians."* Around it stood twelve lesser idols of brass. The spot was called "the plain of kneeling." It had been a favourite resort of King

* Hist. Ireland, p. 156.

Laogaire. To this "Moloch of Ireland" no doubt human victims were sacrificed.

To this plain the ardent missionary bent his way. He resolved that the idol should fall. Romanists differ as to whether it fell at the touch of his "holy staff" or at the voice of his prayer. We believed in neither of these means, for it would involve a miracle. It is far more likely that he caused it to be smitten to the dust by blows which were not at all mysterious. A hammer in a strong hand was sufficient. The people saw that such idols were worse than vanity. There too, it is said, a church was built, transmitting "to succeeding ages the memory of the wonderful things that God had accomplished there by the ministry of his servant."

Another name of the idol is thought to have been *Crom-dubh*, whence a certain day is now called in Ireland, Cromduff Sunday. It may be that the old heathen festival was turned into a Christian observance. The people were not willing to give up, altogether, their pagan revelries, and in their stead certain rites, more Christian, were adopted. It may be that Patrick showed some tolerance toward the old superstitions. He dealt tenderly with the popular usages and prejudices.

He did not break in pieces all the idols of stone, in the spirit of the young Hebrew king, Josiah. The chieftains would not permit it; the clansmen would rise in rebellion. On some of them he was content to inscribe the name of Jesus. Also the wells, which had long been used for heathen purposes, he allowed to be used for baptism. Near them churches were built, so that the people might walk in the old paths for a new purpose. The Druid fire became an Easter flame. In a later day this adaptation of heathen customs to Christian rites gave rise to many evils. Even the good Columba said, without meaning any irreverence, "My Druid is Christ."

"Nothing is clearer," says Dr. O'Donovan, "than that Patrick engrafted Christianity on the pagan superstitions, with so much skill that he won the people over to the Christian religion before they understood the exact difference between the two systems of belief; and much of this half-Pagan, half-Christian religion will be found not only in the Irish stories of the Middle Ages, but in the superstitions of the peasantry to the present day." This is rather a sweeping charge. Without denying that Patrick erred in this direction, it is certainly unfair to lay all these results to his account. Those who came after him were more disposed to compromise with the old Druidic customs. They were ready to borrow from the heathen, as was then done in almost all Christendom. It was this, in a great measure, that made Romanism, and gave it popularity among every people at whose doors the Church's messengers were knocking. Gregory the Great was not a fierce iconoclast. He saw with regret the destruction of heathen temples. "He enjoined their sanctification by Christian rites; the idols only were to be destroyed without remorse. Even the sacrifices of oxen were to continue, but to be celebrated on the saints' days, in order gently to transfer the adoration of the people from their old to their new objects of worship."*

Not yet is the Church rid of this faulty policy. It is rightly felt to be a duty both to Christianize society and to socialize the Church. How shall we adapt our religion to the demands of worldly men? Shall we come down to their tastes, their customs, their habits? Shall we take up what is peculiar to their society and give it a place in the Church? Shall we adopt their amusements and try to hallow them? This will be, not to socialize our Christianity, but to secularize it. It will be to make the

* Milman, Lat. Chris. bk. iii. chap. vii., A. D. 590.

"broad road" the easy avenue to the "strait gate;" the rounds of mirth, the ladder of piety! The apology that such devices will draw some sinners who can be reached by nothing else is suspicious. It reflects on God's own means. His gospel is adapted to reach every soul. To carry into the pulpit the buffooneries that make a street auction interesting to the crowd, all agape for low wit, finds a poor excuse in the assertion that some are thus won who can be gained in no other way. I deny the assertion. So long as men have a conscience and common sense, they can be touched by the solemn realities of eternity and the wondrous love of Christ. The efforts to tempt them into the way of life by worldly lures may afford them amusement, but the result will be only failure. Christ designed that his kingdom should be in the world (not of it), in order to Christianize the world. He did not mean that the world should be brought into his kingdom to secularize that kingdom.

Centres of influence were sought. To gain a country he must win its petty king; the prince first, then the peasantry. Secure the chief, the clan would follow. "To attempt the conversion of the clan in opposition to the will of the chieftain would probably have been to rush upon inevitable death, or at least to risk a violent expulsion from the district." We have seen that such leading men were the first converts. They permitted Patrick to extend his labours. "The clansmen pressed eagerly round the missionary who had baptized the chief, anxious to receive that mysterious initiation into the new faith to which their chieftain and father had submitted. The requirements preparatory to baptism do not seem to have been very rigorous; and it is therefore by no means improbable that in Tirawley and other remote districts, where the spirit of clanship was strong, Patrick, as he tells us himself he did, may have baptized some thousands of men." *

Thus every castle, every court, every city that gave him a footing became a centre of influence, a spring upon the mountain, sending its stream down upon the lowlands. There grew up the central churches, which at length swelled into cathedrals; there were founded the schools, which a later age perverted into monasteries; thence went forth missionaries whose feet were "beautiful upon the mountains," for they were the messengers of "good tidings;" thither resorted young men afterward,

* Todd's St. Patrick, pp. 498, 499.

and changed the old training-schools into rookeries of idle monks.

The love of pioneering was strong in this earnest missionary. To go forth whither none had led the way was his delight. He planted where others should reap. Like Paul, he chose not to build on another man's foundation. No doubt he sought out the scattered bands of believers whom Palladius had failed to visit and strengthen. He may have made their cells the nurseries of schools and churches. In solitary places he may have found a few disciples, who had retreated into the forests to be safe from Druid foes and to hold fellowship with God. These he was able to lead out of their obscure retreats, place them as teachers over bands of youth, or as pastors over little flocks who needed a shepherd.

On his first and perilous journey to the western coast he came upon such a Christian retreat, if we may credit the better lines of an ancient story. There he met the "excellent presbyter Ailbe," who has often been represented as "a bishop" in Ireland before the days of Saint Patrick. The young man is more likely to have been a Culdee missionary. When he was about to be ordained by Patrick, he went to "a cave" and dug from the earth certain glass cups used in the communion service. They were hidden there from intruding robbers, who were very plentiful in those parts. The cave seems to have been a rude chapel, fitted up in a concealed place, a long time before, by some of the early Christians of Ireland. It is pleasant to imagine that Ailbe chose the old retreat as the point for new labours, and won converts from the wild tribes of Sligo, thus building the old waste places and repairing the broken altars of Jehovah.

His enthusiasm for souls was a motive-power within him. He laboured with the ardour and energy of faith, and produced effects upon rude minds which proved that God was with him. Plunging into deep forests as a bold pioneer, he opened the road to Christian civilization. His journeys, if described, would serve as a guide-book to a large part of ancient Ireland. He penetrated the interior. He went down among the Firbolgs of Connaught. He went from one province to another, from one prince to another, undismayed by dangers or difficulties. Like another Paul, he preached the Gospel with the Holy Ghost sent down from heaven; and his labours were crowned with great success. Kings, princes and hostile clans beat their swords into ploughshares and their spears into pruning-hooks; and so abundant was he in labour that in a few years he carried the gospel from Antrim to Kerry, and from the Wicklow mountains to the most secluded glens of Mayo.*

His daring spirit urged him into perilous scenes. What were dangers to such a man? He dared to obey the call of duty. It appears that on a day when he was at Tarah, he overheard two chieftains conversing together about their home and people. One of them said, "I am Enna the son of Amalgaid, from the western regions, where is the Wood of Foclut."

"That seems to be the country of which I had a dream in my youth, where the children called for me to come and help them," answered Patrick; "I will return with you to your home, if the Lord shall so direct."

"Thou shalt not go forth with me, lest we be both slain. It is a long road and beset with enemies."

"Thou mayst never reach thine own country alive unless I go with thee, and, if thou dost not hear my gospel, thou shalt not have eternal life."

"I wish my son to be taught, for he is of tender

* Murray, Ireland and the Irish.

years," said the chief, bringing foward the lad, whom Patrick took by the hand, while a blessing fell from the good man's lips. "But I and my brothers cannot believe until we come to our own people, lest they should mock us."

It was agreed that Patrick should be well guarded upon the rough journey to the far west, "straight across all Ireland." The king sent out a body of men with him, but it appears that the missionary paid fifteen of them for their services. Among some of the wild tribes it seems that the company fell into savage hands, if Patrick wrote the following words: "On that day they most eagerly desired to kill me, but the time was not yet come; yet they plundered everything they found with us, and bound me in irons; but on the fourteenth day the Lord delivered me from their power, and whatever was ours was restored to us, through God and by the help of the close friends whom we had before provided." He seems to have bought his liberty quite often on such occasions, for he adds: "You know how much I expended upon those who were judges throughout all the districts which I used to visit. And I think I paid them the price of not less than fifteen men, that so you might enjoy me, and that I may always enjoy you in the Lord. I do not repent of it, yea it is not enough for me. I still spend and will spend more. The Lord is mighty to give me more hereafter, that I may employ myself for your souls. (2 Cor. xii. 15)."

Crossing the river Moy, he came into a wooded country, like that of which he had dreamed many years before, and which had clung ever since to his imagination. But it quite staggers our faith to read the story of the legend-makers, that he met two young women who were the very children once calling to him from the Focladian forests. We may follow him to the rallying-place of the clan Amalgaid, not far from the present town of Killala. The clansmen had met to elect a leader from among the seven sons of their late chieftain. These sons were brave warriors, "whose match in the field of battle it were difficult to find." One of them was Enna, who had talked with the great missionary at Tarah. Politics ran high, and the candidates for office were not likely to make themselves unpopular. If the people should hear the preacher with favour, the leaders would gladly avow themselves believers. Patrick stood up before the large assembly and declared the glad tidings. "He penetrated the hearts of all," says

Tirechan, "and led them to embrace cordially the Christian faith and doctrine." At an ancient well it is said that large numbers were baptized, and among them the sons of the late chief. Over the flock thus gathered was placed a pastor, "a man of great sanctity, well versed in Holy Scripture."*

The endurances of such a missionary added to his success. Heroism captivates; self-denial carries with it a high degree of reverence. The man who makes sacrifices for a people usually wins their hearts. Monks and Jesuits have ever understood this fact, and when their self-denial was not real, they assumed the guise of it. Their haggard faces, their bare and bleeding feet, won them respect. There is no good proof that Patrick went about in the disguises of poverty and humility. He endured real trials; he made real sacrifices; he refused the offers of gifts and wealth. He was careful to avoid the semblance of seeking his own glory and profit. It is an Irish saying, that if he had accepted all that was offered to him in gratitude, he would not have left as much as would have fed two horses to those who came after him.

From a few lines of the hymn attributed to his disciple Fiacc, whom we saw rising up to honour

* Todd's St. Patrick, pp. 442-449.

him at Tarah, the reader may cull some lines of truth:

> Prudent was Patrick until death:
> Bold was he in banishing error:
> Therefore his fame was extended
> Up to each tribe of the people.
>
> He hymns and revelations
> And the three fifties* sang daily.
> He preached, he prayed, he baptized,
> And from rendering praise never ceased.
>
> He felt not the cold of the season;
> The rains of the night fell upon him:
> To further the kingdom of heaven
> He preached through the day on the hills.
>
> Oft on the bare rock he rested;
> A dampened cloak was his shelter:
> Then, leaving behind his stone pillow,
> He hastened to unceasing labours.†

* *Tres quinquagenas psalmorum* is Colgan's version. This singing of "the three fifties" sounds to us quite as much out of time as if it were said that he took his salary in five-twenties!

† Here we refer to a legend about which some of our readers will be curious to know. It gave rise to a proverb. It is, that when Patrick was in the west of Ireland, he passed his Lent on a high mountain, "fasting forty days without taking any kind of sustenance!" Very wonderful indeed! but Joceline burdens our amazement still more. This monk gravely tells us that "in this place he gathered together the several tribes of serpents and venomous creatures, and drove them headlong into

When some of his "children in the Lord," wishing to show their gratitude, "voluntarily brought him presents, and pious women gladly offered to him their ornaments, Patrick refused them all," in order to avoid the charge that he sought to enrich himself. At first they were offended by his refusal. But they learned to honour him for his rule of not accepting presents for himself. He turned the tide of donations to the Lord. He built up these gifts in walls of schools and churches, or with them "redeemed many Christians from captivity." As a faithful shepherd he was ready to give up everything, even life itself, for the sheep.

In his old age he could appeal to the people, referring to these refusals of gifts: "If I took anything from you, tell me, and I will restore it. Nay, I rather expended money for you, so far as I was able; and I went among you, and everywhere, for your sakes, amid many dangers, even to those extreme regions whither no man had ever gone to the Western ocean, and hence hath proceeded that exemption which Ireland enjoys from all poisonous reptiles." He did it by beating a drum, and this is the only point reasonable in the story. If anything could frighten the "creeping things," a drum would be likely to do it. It must have been some other event that gave to a mountain in that region the name of Croagh-Patrick.

baptize and confirm the people or ordain clergy; and by the help of the Lord I did all things diligently and most gladly for your salvation. At the same time I gave presents to kings, besides the cost of keeping their sons, who walked with me in order that robbers might not seize me and my companions. . . . I call God to witness that I sought not honour from you. That honour is enough for me, which is not seen, but is felt in the heart. [Compare Paul's 'testimony of a good conscience.'] God is faithful, who has promised, and who never lies. But I see myself already, in this world, exalted above measure by the Lord. I know very well that poverty and discomfort suit me much better than riches and a life of pleasure. Yes, indeed; even the Lord Jesus became poor for our sakes. Daily I expected to be seized, dragged into slavery or slain. But I feared none of all these things, for I cast myself in the arms of Him who rules over all, as it written, 'Cast thy burden on the Lord, and he will sustain thee.'"

These are stirring words. They go ploughing through the idle soul, and soften it for fruitfulness. No leisurely bishop was Patrick. Not even could he take time to revisit his native land. "God knows how greatly I have wished it," he is made to say. "I would gladly have gone into Britain, as to my country and parents, and even into Gaul to visit my brethren, and to see the face of the saints of my Lord. But I am bound by the Spirit, who will pronounce me guilty if I do this, and I dread lest the work I have begun should fall to the ground." There is no evidence that he ever left Ireland after he had fully entered upon his mission.

The story that he went to Rome and came back an archbishop is a groundless fiction. If we believe that he went, we may as well take the whole story, and believe that he got some relics for Armagh by rather sharp practice. "While the keepers of the sacred place were asleep and unconscious," he crept in and carried off a goodly quantity of old clothes, blood-stained towels, saints' tresses, and the like. "The pope" winked at the proceeding. "Oh wondrous deed!" exclaims the legendist in rapture. "Oh rare theft of a vast treasure of holy things, committed without sacrilege—the plunder of the most holy place in the world." And yet this writer fails to tell that the pope embraced Patrick, declared him to be the Apostle of Ireland, and made him an archbishop. This invention was left for Joceline.

Attention to young men was a marked feature of the ministry of Patrick. He drew them after him, teaching them as they travelled, and calling out their gifts by employing them in the good work. Certain chieftains allowed their sons to attend him, often at his expense. The gentle lad Benignus, the charming singer, was long at his side. When he found men of the lower rank suited to a higher calling, he took care to have them instructed and fitted to become teachers of the people. Thus he was raising up a native ministry.

The redemption of captives was another feature of his wise policy. He had "a zeal to preserve the country where he himself had borne the yoke from the abuses of slavery, and especially from the incursions of the pirates—Britons and Scots, robbers and traffickers in men—who made it a sort of store from which they took their human cattle."* This gave him favour with the peasantry, who loved their children equally with the nobles in their forts and castles. Many of the rescued captives seem to have been placed in schools and trained for the work of teaching and preaching. It was common at that time in Europe for the

---

* Montalembert, Monks of the West, vol. ii. p. 392.

missionaries to purchase heathen slaves, educate them, and send them back to their native land to bear the tidings of salvation. Patrick was an example to himself of what a redeemed captive might accomplish.

To do and suffer all in the name of the Lord appears to have been Patrick's earnest desire. For him he could labour, suffer, die. He was willing to be counted as one of the "least of all saints." He says, " Let none think that I place myself on a level with the apostles. I am a poor, sinful, despicable man. . . . Ye fine talkers, who know nothing of the Lord, learn who it is that has called a simple person like myself from the ranks of the lowly to serve this people, to whom the love of Christ has led me. . . . I have no power unless he gives it to me. He knows that I greatly desire that he would give me the cup of suffering which he has given others to drink. I pray God that he would give me perseverance, and think me worthy to bear a faithful testimony until the time of my departure. If I have striven to do anything for the sake of my God whom I love, I beseech him to allow me to shed my blood for his name, with those of my new converts who have been cast into prison, even should I obtain no burial, or should my body be torn in pieces by wild beasts. I firmly believe that if this should happen to me, I have gained my soul along with my body; for beyond a doubt we shall rise again in that day with the splendour of the sun; that is, with the glory of our Redeemer. . . . The sun which we see daily rises and sets; but the sun Christ will never set, nor will those who do his will. They shall live, as Christ lives, for ever."

The power of prayer was held to be an essential means of success. Not only did Patrick entreat God with fervour, but he laboured to secure a praying Church. In the old Culdee spirit he chose cells and secluded places for supplication. Thither he wished the people to resort. There they might renew their strength. Thence they might go into the great field, with the blessing of the Lord upon them and the Spirit burning in their hearts. It was hardly his design to found monasteries. "Saint Patrick had a much higher object in view. He seems to have been deeply imbued with faith in the intercessory powers of the Church. He established throughout the land temples and oratories [praying-places] for the perpetual worship of God. He founded societies of priests and bishops, whose first duty it was 'to make constant supplications, prayers, intercessions, and giving thanks for all men.'" He felt that without prayer his preaching would be in vain. From this source slowly arose an evil. These societies became convents in a later century. It would be too much, probably, to claim that Patrick was entirely free from the monastic tendencies of that age, yet he was not a monk. His effort was not to found monasteries.

The power of God was the great cause of success. To secure it, all else was done. It came by prayer, by faithful preaching of the divine word, and by the agencies of active laymen and teachers. Men planted, God gave the harvest.

Early in Ireland, Christianity took a somewhat national form. It was not looked upon as coming from foreigners, nor did it adopt a foreign character. It had peculiarities of its own. "The successors of Saint Patrick in his missionary labours were many of them descendants of the ancient kings and chieftains so venerated by a clannish people. The surrounding chieftains and men in authority, who still kept aloof in paganism, were softened by degrees when they perceived that in all the assemblies of the Christian Church fervent prayers were offered to God for them. In this point of view the public incense of prayer and 'lifting up of hands' of the Church in a heathen land is perhaps the most important engine of missionary success. 'Nothing,' says St. Chrysostom, 'is so apt to draw men under teaching as to love and to be loved;' to be prayed for in the spirit of love." * We do not need for this purpose any other societies than the churches of the land; no convents, no monasteries, but bands of Christians earnest in prayer, in their homes and in the house of God.

Persecution was the usual attendant of missionary effort in a heathen country. Christian civilization has generally followed in the footsteps of a bleeding Church. But the early Christians of Ireland were not exposed so much to the sword, the rack and the flames. Still their peace has been exaggerated. "While, in other countries," says Mr. Moore, "the introduction of Christianity has been the slow work of time, has been resisted by either government or people, and seldom effected without a lavish effusion of blood, in Ireland, on the contrary, by the influence of one humble but zealous missionary, and with little previous preparation of the soil by other hands, Christianity burst forth at the first ray of apostolic light and with the sudden ripeness of a northern summer, and at once covered

* Todd's St. Patrick, p. 514.

the whole land. Kings and princes, when not themselves among the ranks of the converted, saw their sons and daughters joining in the train without a murmur. Chiefs, at variance in all else, agreed in meeting beneath the Christian banner; and the proud Druid and bard laid their superstitions meekly at the foot of the Cross; nor, by a singular disposition of Providence, unexampled indeed in the whole history of the Church, was there a single drop of blood shed, on account of religion, through the entire course of this mild Christian revolution, by which, in the space of a few years, all Ireland was brought tranquilly under the influence of the gospel." *

This pleasing picture is not true to fact. Not all Ireland was converted, even nominally. Very much was done, but not without the shedding of a drop of Christian blood. Patrick refers to his brethren who suffered and were slain for their faith. His own life was always in danger and often assailed. We have seen him going westward with an escort, and even then he did not escape injury. He had some of his schools and churches encircled by walls and fortifications for the protection of the inmates. The great churches stood as the castles of Christ.

* Hist. Ireland, i. p. 203.

A touching story is told of Oran, his charioteer. Patrick had overturned the great black stone, the idol of the Irish, and he was travelling into Leinster. For this deed a certain chief, named Berraid, sought revenge. He resolved to fall upon him if Patrick ever passed by his fortress. This resolution came to the ear of Oran, who seems to have been in the habit of walking beside the gig, that may have had but one seat. When they came near the castle, Oran pretended to be very weary, and his master gave up the seat and took the road on foot. Soon the plotting chieftain hurled a javelin at the man who was riding past, taking him for the image-breaker. Oran fell mortally wounded, but in dying had the satisfaction of having saved the life of the master whom he loved by the sacrifice of his own.

The Leinster men seem to have shown especial aversion to Patrick and his doctrines. They had driven away Palladius, and their sleeping wrath was easily aroused. It is told by the later writers that Patrick went into this province, hoping first to win Dunlaing the king, and then the people. He visited the royal castle of Naas. Two of the king's sons accepted the gospel. This provoked the sullen and crafty Foillen, one of the royal officers. He laid his plans to rid the court of the hated teacher of religion. On a day when he saw Patrick coming to talk with him he pretended to be asleep. The visitor entered the room, but detected the plot to take his life. The wicked man was disarmed, and probably was secretly thrown into a prison, where he soon died. This is more likely than that his feigned repose proved the sleep of death, as the legend-makers affirm. But the idea went out among the people that on the approach of Patrick his eyes were sealed for ever in death, and hence the proverb, used when a Leinster man wishes his worst to an enemy: "May his sleep be like that of Foillen in the castle of Naas."

CHAPTER XI.

PATRICK'S CREED.

THE articles of a great man's faith may interest us quite as much as the acts of his life. If his belief was sound, his example will have more force. Saint Patrick lived in an age when eminent men were expected to announce their creed. He wrote none. This may go to show that then Ireland was not troubled with the great questions which agitated the Continent. On that isle, in the north-west of Christendom, no footing was given to the heresies of Pelagius, who denied man's native helplessness; and Arius, who denied the divinity of Christ. It may show that Patrick had no contact with the Roman world.

But Patrick strongly expressed his doctrines. We may gather them from the writings which pass under his name. They crop out like the granite in a mountain land. When he pleads or rebukes, or tells the simple story of his life, they gleam forth as gems washed up by the waves. In his warmest sentences he drives a nail that shines with

Scripture. And it is worthy of notice that he does not quote the version of Jerome, which was largely used in the Roman churches. He quotes the old Latin Vulgate,* such a translation as he would likely have found in a Culdee cell if he was there as a student in his earlier days. The Bible of a man's youth is preferred in his old age.

All that has come down to us from his pen, except the hymn, was written in the evening of his life. He could look back upon the great work done in a vast field. The glory of God was dear to his heart; to live for that was his motive. Tillemont says of the Confession: "It was written to give glory to God for the great grace which the author had received, and to assure the people of his mission that it was indeed God himself who had sent him to preach to them the gospel, to strengthen their faith, and to make known to all the world that the desire of preaching the gospel, and of having a part in its promises, was the sole motive which had induced him to go to Ireland. He had long intended to write, but had deferred doing so, fearing lest what he wrote should be ill-received among men because he had not learned to write well, and what he had learned of Latin

---

* Todd's St. Patrick, pp. 347–349.

was still further corrupted by intermixture with the Irish language. . . . The work is full of good sense, and even of intellect and fire, and, what is better, it is full of piety. The saint exhibits throughout the greatest humility, without lowering the dignity of his ministry. We see in the tract much of the character of St. Paul. The author was undoubtedly well read in the Scriptures." *
He expected that it would be read by better scholars than himself; perhaps there were such in Ireland, even among the students whom he had trained.

Patrick tells us: "I am greatly a debtor to God, who hath vouched me such great grace that many people by my means should be born again to God; and that clergy should be ordained everywhere for the people who have lately come to the faith; for the Lord hath taken them from the ends of the earth, as he has promised of old by his prophets: 'The Gentiles shall come to thee from the ends of the earth, and shall say, Surely our fathers have inherited lies and vanity, and there is no profit in them.' And again: 'I have given thee as a light to the Gentiles, that thou mayest be for salvation, even unto the end of the earth.' And there I

* Tillemont, Mem. Eccl. S. Patrick, xvi. p. 461.

desire to wait for the promise of him who never faileth; as he promiseth in his gospel: 'They shall come from the east, and from the west, and shall sit down with Abraham, and Isaac, and Jacob;' as we believe that believers shall come from the whole world."

The results of his work appeared astonishing as he reviewed it: " Whence comes it that in Hiberio* those who never had any knowledge of God, and up to the present time worshipped only idols and abominations, are lately become the people of the Lord, and are called the sons of God? The sons of Scots† and daughters of Christians appear now as monks and virgins of Christ—even one blessed Scottish lady, of noble birth and of great beauty, who was adult, and whom I baptized." Who this lady was we know not, but we are told that, of her own accord, she devoted herself to a more secluded life in order to "live nearer to God." Others did the same, even at the cost of enduring persecution from their nearest relatives.

His thoughts took somewhat the form of a creed when writing of the great benefits that God

---

* His name for Ireland.

† The Northern Irish were called Scots. The references to *monks* will be explained hereafter.

gave him in the land of his captivity. He says: "After we have been converted and brought to God we should exalt and confess his wondrous works before every nation under the whole heaven, that *there is none other God,* nor ever was, nor shall be hereafter, than *God the Father* unbegotten, without beginning, from whom is all beginning, upholding all things.

"*And his Son Jesus Christ*, whom we acknowledge to have been always with the Father before the beginning of the world, spiritually with the Father, in an ineffable manner begotten, before all beginning; and by him were all things made, visible and invisible.

"*And being made man,* and having overcome death, he was received into heaven unto the Father; and [the Father] hath given unto him all power, above every name, of things in heaven and things in earth, and things under the earth, that every tongue should confess that Jesus Christ is Lord and God;

"Whom we believe and *look for his coming;* who is soon about to be the Judge of quick and dead; who will render unto every man according to his work;

"And who hath poured into us abundantly *the*

gift of the Holy Ghost, and the pledge of immortality; who maketh the faithful and obedient to become the sons of God the Father, and joint heirs with Christ;

" Whom we confess and worship, *one God in the Trinity of the Sacred Name.*"

Such is the brief summary of doctrines in the Confession. It was not intended to be a full creed. We shall find in the Epistle to Coroticus a hearty expression of other doctrines, so uttered that they might burn upon the consciences of bad men or be a comfort to certain disciples in captivity.

It appears that one evening there was a multitude witnessing a baptism. A goodly number of converts, clad in white robes, were at the fountain. The minister, who seems not to have been Patrick, was baptizing them. Very soon after a band of pirates rushed upon them. Some were slain while the drops of water were scarcely dried from their foreheads. Others were carried away in their white robes. The people were affrighted and ran for their lives. Houses were plundered and almost every sort of outrage committed. The captives were taken to the sea-shore, put into boats, borne away to a foreign land and sold into slavery. The man who did this act of villainy, or in whose name it was done, was Coroticus. He seems to have been a petty prince of Wales, perhaps Caradoc, from whom the county of Cardigan is said to derive its name. Some of the Scots and Picts seem to have aided in the nefarious business.

The heart of Patrick was touched with pity for the captives, and filled with indignation against the marauders. He wrote a protest against the merciless deed. He chose wise and earnest men and sent them to the cruel prince. One of them he calls "a venerable presbyter, whom I taught from infancy." He must have been worthy of the delicate mission. Perhaps he was Benignus. Taking their boat, these men went to Coroticus, who professed to be a Christian! They presented the letter of the man who styled himself "Bishop in Ireland."

"What right has he to reprove me?" we hear the prince say haughtily. "He is not my bishop."

"But have mercy on the poor people," is the entreaty of the venerable presbyter. "Be so good as to restore some of the plunder and set free the baptized captives."

"Away with you!" we seem to hear the lawless chieftain reply. "They were all taken by the rights of war. It is too late to plead for them; they have been sold, and I have the money for them. Get you gone! You Irish are fit only to be slaves. In five minutes I'll put chains about your necks, offer you in the market and find what you are worth."

"God will bring you into judgment—"

"Away, away! Officers, take these insolent Irishmen out of my presence."

In some such manner the embassy was dismissed with scoffs and ridicule. Contempt was thrown upon the letter of Patrick, which has not been preserved. The wise men had to return, carrying only disappointment to many parents and relatives, who had hoped to see the boats returning loaded with their goods, their children and their friends.

Again Patrick took his pen. He wrote another protest. He sent it out into the world, hoping that it would drop down like a shaft of lightning upon Coroticus, and drift as an olive branch to the captives. He says: "It is the custom of the Roman and Gallican Christians to raise large sums of money for the redemption of baptized captives from the Franks and other pagans. But you, a professing Christian, slay the disciples of Christ or you sell them to heathen nations. You hand over the members of Christ to the abominations of the heathen."

Then addressing the hirelings of the chieftain, he says: "Patrick, an ignorant sinner, and yet appointed a bishop in Hibernia, and dwelling among the barbarous tribes because of my love to God, I write these letters with my own hand to be borne to the soldiers of the tyrant: I say not to my fellow-citizens, nor to the fellow-citizens of the Roman saints, but to the co-workers of the devil, as their evil deeds prove. For they live in death; they are the associates of the apostate Scots and Picts; they fatten on the blood of innocent Christians, multitudes of whom I have begotten and confirmed in Christ. . . . Does not the divine mercy which I cherish oblige me to defend even those who once made me a captive, and put to the massacre the servants of my father? For this people are confessing their sins and turning to the Lord. Let your souls melt when I praise the courage of the girls whom you insulted and stole away. Those delicate children of mine in the faith, how they defended themselves from outrage! What heroic courage against their unworthy masters!

"The Church weeps and wails over her sons and over her daughters, whom the sword has not yet slain, but who are exiled in far-off lands where sin openly and shamelessly abounds. There Christian freemen are reduced to slavery, and that by the most unworthy, most infamous and apostate Picts. O most beauteous and beloved children! I can but cry out to you; I cannot tell what to do with you; I am not worthy to give help. The wickedness of the wicked hath prevailed over us. We are become as aliens. Do they believe that you and us have received one baptism, that we have one God, our Father? Perhaps not; with them it is a crime that we [ye] are born in Hibernia. . .*

" Have ye not one God? Why then wrong one another? I grieve for myself. But yet I rejoice that I have not laboured in vain; not in vain hath been my pilgrimage here; only there hath come to pass this outrage so horrible and unspeakable.

" Thanks be to God, O ye believers and baptized [ye who have been slain]! ye have gone from this world to Paradise. I behold you. You have begun to journey whither there shall be no night, nor sorrow nor death: ye shall exult as lambs let loose:

* " If Coroticus had at that time succeeded in banishing the Gwyddil, or Irish settlers in South Wales, and in the frenzy of victory had pursued them to Ireland, it is not unnatural that his followers should regard every native of Ireland as an enemy, and treat him as such." In his sympathy Patrick identifies himself with the captives.—*Todd, St. Patrick,* 360.

ye shall trample upon the ungodly; they shall be as ashes under your feet. Ye shall reign with apostles and prophets and martyrs. Ye shall receive everlasting kingdoms. . . . Without are dogs and sorcerers and murderers and liars, whose portion is the lake of eternal fire. . . .

"Thus shall sinners and the ungodly perish from the face of the Lord; but the righteous, in great joy, shall feast with Christ, shall judge the heathen, and shall rule over ungodly kings for ever and ever. . . .

"I testify before God and his holy angels, that it shall be so as my ignorance* has said. These are not my words; they are the words of God, of his apostles and prophets, who never lie. I have translated them into Latin.† They who believe shall be saved, but whoso believeth not shall be damned. God hath spoken. I therefore earnestly request of every one who may become the bearer of this letter, that it be withheld from none, but let it be read before all the people, and in the pres-

---

* *Mea imperita*, that is, "I myself." It was the frequent mode of speaking with this humble man. He is concluding the epistle.

† Had he consulted the original tongues, so as to be sure of the meaning, and then made a new translation?

ence of Coroticus himself. May God inspire them to return to a better mind toward him, so that even, though late, they may repent of their impious deeds. They have been the murderers of the brethren of the Lord. But let them repent and set free the baptized captive women. Thus shall God count them worthy of life, and they shall be made whole here and for ever. Peace* to the Father, to the Son and to the Holy Ghost. Amen."

Thus closes the stirring letter; now revealing flashes of lightning, and again the gentle sunbeams of love. Its effect we know not. The proud chieftain was worthy of only the silence of history. No return is mentioned of a single captive. Bondage was to them a severe school, but it was the school of God. It may have been blessed to them as it had once been to the great and good man who had brought the gospel to their native land. It may have waked them to a higher life. Perhaps their baptism had been little more than outward and nominal—a thing too common throughout Christen-

---

* Perhaps he meant "glory," or he may have meant it as a prayer that Coroticus might repent and find peace with God. No revenge burns in the noble epistle: with all his tremendous voice of justice Patrick breathed the invitations of mercy. Here was love to an enemy.

dom in that age. It had ushered them into the Church; but now they may feel the need of "the washing of regeneration;" now they may seek union with Christ. Perhaps many of them were a blessing to others. Some little maiden may have proved as an angel unawares in the house of a Pictish Naaman. Some youth may have thought how Ireland once had a slave who had become her spiritual deliverer; and why might not the captive among a barbarous people serve the Lord so well that his master should ask the way of happiness and life? Bondsmen have been employed by the Redeemer to set nations free.

CHAPTER XII.

THE CHURCH OF SAINT PATRICK.

WHAT was the Church built up by Saint Patrick? its form, its offices, its term of existence? To this inquiry we set ourselves in the interest of historic truth, and not in that of any party. Christ was more to him than the Church; of the one we know what he believed—of the other it is hard to learn what he thought. He was not the high churchman of any denomination.

The late Dr. Murray well said: "There has been much learned and rather sharp controversy as to the polity or external form of the Church in the days of Patrick. The Prelatists claim him as archbishop, as having received orders in a direct line from the apostles, and as thus transmitting orders to them. To believe this leads necessarily to the belief of the monkish fables in reference to him. This claim it is impossible to establish, whether it be true or false in itself. Some Independents would claim him as a noble Congregationalist; among whom, we believe, stands the eloquent and warm-hearted Mr. King, of Dublin; whilst others, of the Belfast school, would claim him as a Presbyterian. That he was not a Papist is certain; but what he was in polity is very uncertain. It is most likely he troubled himself far less upon that subject than do many in our day, esteeming it his great work to preach the gospel. But when we read that 'Ireland was full of village bishops'—that in one county, Meath, there were nearly thirty bishops—that at one period there were about three hundred bishops in the kingdom, we may reasonably conclude that parochial bishops were the only ones known to the primitive Christianity of Ireland, and that every parish was a bishopric. But there is darkness sufficient resting upon the annals of those early times to forbid dogmatism on the one hand, and there are now and then the gleaming out of great principles sufficient to form the basis of theories on the other."*

We have seen young men following Patrick as students and helpers. Thus they were trained for missionary work. It was not necessary to send them far away to the Continent to be educated, where the system of schools was becoming mo-

---

* Ireland and the Irish.

nastic. There were places for retired study at home. The old Culdee system had its cells, which grew into colleges. There is reason to think that Patrick found this system in Ireland and adopted its main features. The cell, or *kil*, seems to have been at first a refuge from danger and a resort for prayer; then a fixed abode for studious men. It grew into a church or a college; often it became a religious centre, whither the people flocked for worship, teaching and consolation. In the course of years a town grew up around many a prominent cell. We find very many names as memorials of the ancient *kil;* such as Kildare, the church or cell of the oak; Kill-fine, the church of the tribe; Cill-Chiarain, the cell of Ciaran, or Kieran.

The story of Ciaran is that he went into a dense wood of Munster, made him a cell, played with the wild animals around him, studied and lived near to God. He drew to him young men of serious minds and taught them; the school enlarged into a monastery; a city arose on the spot. It is not certain when he lived. Some make him a bishop in Ireland thirty years before Saint Patrick; others, a child to whom the great missionary gave his blessing on one of his journeys; and others place him in the sixth century.

Here is probably a specimen of the schools in the days of Saint Patrick. The students were called monks because they led a secluded life. But a young monk of the fifth century was a very different man from an old monk of the twelfth century. He was usually a young man preparing to become a missionary. His head was shorn, and he wore a dress peculiar to his class. If he grew too fond of a secluded life, he remained at the cell for long years, or he went forth into the forests to found one for himself. This often occurred in later times. But we do not think Saint Patrick allowed such men to take their rest. They must prepare for work in the world, and when prepared go forth into the great field to sow and reap for the Master.

It appears that Patrick often visited these schools, which ought not be called monasteries.

The regulations were very different from monastic rules. They were little else than would now be demanded in a college where the inmates were required to support themselves. "Although they observed a certain institute," says Jamieson, "yet, in the accounts given of them, we cannot overlook this remarkable distinction between them and those societies which are properly monastic, that they were not associated for the purpose of observing this rule. They might deem certain regulations necessary for the preservation of order, but their great design was, by communicating instruction, to train up others for the work of the ministry. Hence it has been justly observed that they may be more properly viewed as colleges, in which various branches of useful learning were taught, than as monasteries. These societies, therefore, were in fact the seminaries of the Church both in North Britain and in Ireland."*

When Patrick found in these schools men qualified for the work, he was ready to say, "The Lord hath need of thee." He had the care of churches that needed pastors. He ordained them as bishops. Thus he laid his hands on the gentle Benignus and placed him over the church of Armagh. There the good pastor fed the flock for many years. He travelled widely, and gave "splendid proofs of his zeal for religion and his anxious desire for the conversion of his countrymen." But he went to his rest a few years before the great man who had led him forth from his father's house when a youth. There is nothing but manufactured evidence to show that he ever

* Jamieson, Hist. Culdees, p. 33.

had charge of more than one church, or that he had a diocese and an array of clergy under him.

Thus, too, Patrick, when travelling along the banks of the Liffey, came upon Fiacc, whom he had once met as a young bard at the court of Tarah. The poet had been studying for the ministry. He was ordained a bishop and placed over the church of Sletty. At a later day imagination set him over all Leinster. He, no doubt, had a general interest in the little bands of Christians in that region, and made many a missionary tour, as many a zealous pastor now does in a new country. But this does not prove that he had a diocese. He seems to have been a good husband, a kind father, a learned man and the teacher of many disciples. It does not appear that he persuaded his former tutor, Dubtach, the converted bard, to preach the gospel. But this eminent man breathed into Celtic poetry the name of Christ. Druid songs were changed to Christian hymns. The pagan lyre became a solemn psaltery, giving its notes to holy psalms. An old author says that when once blessed and transformed, the songs of the bards became so sweet that the angels of God leaned down from heaven to listen; and this is why the harp of the bards has continued to be the symbol and emblazonry of Ireland.

When we go back as nearly as history will carry us to the days of Saint Patrick, we find that the weight of evidence justifies the following conclusions:

1. Men were ordained bishops *per saltum*, that is, without passing through other clerical orders. They had not first to be deacons and priests.* A young man might be ordained a bishop, just as now a student is ordained a presbyter, thus given the highest office known to Presbyterianism.

2. Men were thus ordained by a single bishop. It seems that Patrick often used this power alone. It began as a necessity, perhaps, when he was the only bishop in Ireland, and was continued after his example. But this may not have been the only rule of ordination. Even if it were, it would not be against one form of church government more than another, for in no Church is it allowable for one bishop to ordain another, whatever may be understood by that title of office.

3. Men were ordained bishops without being placed over any particular church. They had not the oversight of churches or clergy. They were evangelists, missionaries, travelling preachers and

* Todd's St. Patrick, ch. i.; which may be consulted on most of the following points.

superintendents of schools. It is admitted by Prelatists that they were "bishops without sees or dioceses—wandering bishops." This class became very numerous in Ireland.

Early in the twelfth century, Anselm of England complained thus of the state of affairs in Ireland: "It is said that bishops in your country are elected at random, and appointed without any fixed place of episcopal jurisdiction; and that a bishop, like a priest, is ordained by a single bishop." Such had been the state of things since the time of Patrick, who was eager to have a strong force of missionaries in the field; and he thought it important for them to hold the highest office and be the equal of himself. It cannot be shown that he was ever anything but a "bishop in Ireland," as he styled himself in his last days.

4. A single church had its bishop; probably every church had one of its own. St. Bernard in the twelfth century thought this one sign of "a making void of religion," that "every particular church should have its particular bishop." But Patrick held a different view. His rule seems to have been to place over every church a pastor, who was in office equal to himself. Hence Nennius says that he founded three hundred and sixty-five

churches, and placed over them three hundred and sixty-five bishops.

5. The bishops outnumbered the churches. "It is, therefore, an undoubted fact," says Dr. Todd, "that the number of bishops in Ireland was very great in early times, in proportion to the population, as well as absolutely; although we are not bound to believe that Saint Patrick consecrated 'with his own hand' three hundred and fifty bishops, founded seven hundred churches and ordained three thousand priests."

Nor are we bound to believe that there were so many places as are reported where seven bishops dwelt together as a brotherhood. Probably there were a few such in a later century, but hardly one hundred and forty-one of them! Nine hundred and eighty-seven bishops thus taking their ease! The monkish annalists were death upon prelatic theories.

"There is abundant evidence," says Dr. Todd, "to show that two or more contemporary bishops frequently lived together during the early period [of the Irish Church], in the same town, church or monastery." But this was doubtless some centuries after Patrick's death, when the monastic system was in full vigour. In his day the settled and travelling bishops seemed to have been greater in number than the churches. Of the latter it is not possible to make any estimate.

6. The bishop had no diocese. He was a pastor or missionary. In the afternoon of the sixth century it was enough for Columba to be ordained a bishop in order to qualify him for the great work before him in Scotland. Nor was any higher office ever conferred upon him. So Columban, who went into Europe, is called by the same author a presbyter, and in another sentence a bishop, as if they were the very same office. The bishops who are represented to have been placed over dioceses by Patrick belong to a later day. Even the four whom some have thought preceded him, and others to have laboured with him, seem to belong to the sixth or seventh century. They were Ciaran, Ailbe, Ibar and Declan. Perhaps the first two were coworkers of Patrick. Montalembert admits that "the constitution of dioceses and parishes, in Ireland as in Scotland, does not go farther back than to the twelfth century."

7. Patrick was a "bishop in Ireland," and not the primate over it. He had upon him, in a very important sense, "the care of all the churches," quite as Calvin had a general superintendence of all the

Protestant churches of France. But was Calvin an archbishop? He was a presbyter, the equal only in office of his brethren.

It was very easy for writers, centuries after Patrick's time, to represent the great central churches as diocesan, the prominent pastors as prelatic bishops, the schools as monasteries, female teachers as the founders of nunneries, and over them all one great chief, one archbishop, Saint Patrick. But of all this we do not believe a word. The old Irish term *ard-epscop* only meant an eminent or celebrated bishop, as *ard-file* meant a chief poet, or *ard-righ*, an eminent king. It did not signify an archbishop in the modern sense.* It might have been applied to any well-known and influential pastor.

We may well believe that several synods were held by Patrick and his co-presbyters. But it is very doubtful whether he published any "canons" over his name; certainly not the collections as they now appear. If he wrote any laws for the Church, the Romanists of a later age foisted in certain rules to serve their purpose. Thackeray says of the canons of the first synod, held about the year 460, "Although some marks of superstition may be

* Todd's St. Patrick, p. 16.

traced in them, and some leaning to the Church of Rome, we cannot help being struck by the simplicity, force and sense which pervade them."* The striking parts may have come from Patrick, the rest from those who meddled with all that he left behind him.

It is in connection with some of these supposed synods that we hear of Auxilius and Iserninus. The story is, that they came as bishops to assist Patrick. Who sent them is not told in the Ulster Annals. The later account is that they went from Rome with him to Ireland. If their Roman mission has no better foundation than his, we may give little credit to their existence, and yet not be guilty of taking their lives.

Patrick must have had a very great influence over the Irish Church. He had a splendid gift of management. He was able to keep all the forces at work. Whatever his official power, there is no proof that he gave any account of his use of it to the court of Rome. "He did not apply to the papal see to have the election of the bishops appointed by him confirmed; nor is there extant any rescript from the 'apostolic' see to him, or any epistle to Rome. . . . We have no record or hint of

* Anc. Brit. ii. p. 167.

his having kept up any communication with Rome." We are quoting a writer, who thinks that the existence of so many missionary and pastor-bishops in the early Irish Church was an error, yet he says, "It was an error into which a very zealous man, who thought he could not have enough of chief pastors and shepherds of Christ's flock was likely to fall; but it was one that could not for a moment have been tolerated by Rome. Had she known it [or had any right to rule], she would doubtless have immediately put a stop to such an irregularity. The obvious inference is, that she was not made acquainted with the state of the infant Church in Ireland, and therefore that St. Patrick acted independently of the papal authority."* In order to explain this it has been assumed that he had no need to give an account of himself, for "he was made apostolic legate over Ireland." But St. Bernard informs us that "Gillebert, bishop of Limerick, in the twelfth century, was the first who discharged the duties of apostolic legate in Ire-

* Rev. W. G. Todd, Church of St. Patrick, pp. 29-36. Mr. Todd has fully examined the subject, and he also says: "I have not been able to discover any fair instance of a bishop being elected to an Irish see by the interference of the pope, from the mission of St. Patrick until after the English invasion." See also Lanigan, ii. 170.

land." Thus falls to the ground the claim that Patrick acted in the name or interest of Rome.

There is some reason to think that the Church of Saint Patrick was more nearly presbyterial than congregational or prelatic. It was certainly not papal. It gradually adopted many errors, but it did not submit to the Pope of Rome until the twelfth century.

It grew, extended and became a vast power in the world. Its schools became justly renowned. They attracted students from distant realms. The pupils of a single school were often numbered by thousands. The course of instruction embraced all the sciences then taught, but more especially the study of the Holy Scriptures.

Thus the work of church extension, commenced on a large scale by Patrick, was carried on by faithful followers, until, before the beginning of the ninth century, the whole land had been studded with churches, colleges and scriptural schools, and Irish Christians were famous over Europe for learning, piety and missionary zeal. The Irish, who still were known by the name of Scots, were the only divines who refused to dishonour their reason by submitting it implicitly to the dictates of authority. Naturally subtle and sagacious, they applied their philosophy, such as it was, to the illustration of the truths and doctrines of religion—a method which was almost generally abhorred and exploded in all the nations. They were lovers of learning, and distinguished themselves, in these times of ignorance, by the culture of the sciences, beyond all other European nations. Owing to the eminence of the Irish in science and literature, and to the steadfastness with which they held fast the profession of their faith without wavering, Ireland was regarded at this period, throughout Europe, as the school of the West and an isle of saints.*

Camden says: "The Saxons of that age flocked thither, as to the great mart of learning, and this is the reason why we find this saying so often in our [English] writers, 'Such an one was sent over into Ireland to be educated.'† No wonder that Aldhelm, abbot of Malmesbury, exclaimed, in a letter to Ealfrid, who had spent six years studying in Ireland, 'Why should Ireland, whither students are transported in troops by fleets, be exalted with such unspeakable advantages?'"

The rapid extension and singular prosperity of the early Irish Church is to be attributed, in no

---

* Mosheim, Eccl. Hist. Cent. ix.; Ussher, chap. vi.
† Britannia, Art. Ireland.

small degree, to its freedom from foreign control, and to the excellence of its system of church government. "Bishops were appointed without consulting Rome. They consecrated bishops for foreign missions; and these missions, in many instances, opposed the mandates of Rome. For more than five centuries after the death of St. Patrick we scarcely have any vestiges of a connection between Rome and Ireland. Councils and synods were held from time to time, in order to bring the Church of Ireland to the same subordination to Rome as those of every other part of Europe."* It is thus evident that in things spiritual and ecclesiastical they refused obedience alike to pope and king, holding that *the Lord Jesus Christ is sole King and head of His Church.*

It would require a volume to do justice to the foreign missions of the Church of Saint Patrick. We should have to follow Columba, as he revived the system of the Culdees in Scotland, and made Iona a great northern light casting its rays over all

* O'Halloran. Rev. W. G. Todd, a prelatist, in his *Church of St. Patrick*, furnishes satisfactory evidence that the bishop of Rome did not appoint, elect, consecrate, nor confirm the bishops of Ireland, from the fifth to the twelfth century; nor did he sanction the missions of the Irish Church, of which that of Columba was the first, to another country.

Europe. We should have to trace Columban and Gallus marching, with weary feet, through Gaul, up the Rhine, over the Alps or into Italy, founding monasteries, rearing churches, enduring storm and cold, persecuted by kings and lifting neglected tribes out of barbarism. We should find Virgilius at Salzburg, in the far-off wilds of the Tyrol, not only teaching the gospel, but also watching the motions of the planets and concluding that the earth was round, and that on the other side, beneath his feet, there might be nations of men. His doctrine of the antipodes brought him into trouble with the pope. We have scarcely begun the list. In the year 565 the first missionary left the shores of Ireland. For nearly three centuries companies of learned and pious men, from the colleges of Ireland, continued to go forth to preach Christ in the neighbouring countries. In North and South Britain, and over all the Continent, they went everywhere preaching the gospel. Rejecting purgatory, the worship of images, the intercession of saints, and transubstantiation—doctrines unknown in the Church of St. Patrick, and only recently introduced into the Church of Rome—they were always opposed by the Roman Catholic clergy, and often suffered persecution; still they held fast the truth, and continued, till 840, to preach to the inhabitants of Continental Europe the very same Gospel preached by St. Patrick to the wondering natives of Ireland.*

Concerning the theology of this period Neander writes: "In the Irish Church, from the time of its origin, a bolder spirit of inquiry had been propagated, which caused many a reaction against the papacy; and as in the Irish monasteries, not only the Latin, but also the Greek fathers had been studied, so it naturally came about that from that school issued a more original and free development of theology than was to be elsewhere found, and was thence propagated to other lands."

In the year 807 the Danes invaded Ireland. They were a fierce and warlike people, and treated the vanquished with horrid cruelty. Themselves worshippers of heathen gods, they considered it a religious duty to exterminate the Christians. For two hundred years the Irish were engaged in deadly conflict with these savage hordes. In the beginning of the eleventh century the storm subsided. There was a temporary calm. But already two centuries of civil war had produced their melancholy results. The great schools and colleges

* Wilson, Church of St. Patrick, p. 59.

had been plundered, burned, and their inmates slaughtered or dispersed. The churches were in ruins and the flocks scattered. The national records and many ancient documents deposited in the monasteries had perished in the flames; the bonds of society were loosened and social anarchy prevailed. Though learning and religion speedily revived, and schools and churches began to rise from their ashes, yet, owing to disunion and many irregularities, the Irish were less able than before to resist the insidious inroads of papal influence.

The Romish bishops of the Danes in Ireland used all their influence to induce the native Irish to adopt Roman Catholic doctrines and modes of worship, and to acknowledge the authority of the Roman pontiff. When it is remembered how completely the early Irish Church had been disorganized by two centuries of civil war, it will not seem strange that many of its members proved unfaithful to the old religion of their fathers, and accepted the new doctrines of Rome, lately brought into Ireland by these foreign bishops. Thus the Irish Church fell away from her ancient faith, and before a century had elapsed measures were taken to deprive her of her ancient independence.*

* Church of St. Patrick, pp. 60–67.

The English invaded and took possession of Ireland in the year 1172. No sooner had the pope heard of the success of the English expedition than he wrote to King Henry a letter of congratulation. "It is not (he wrote) without very lively sensations of satisfaction that we have learned of the expedition you have made in the true spirit of a pious king against the nation of the Irish, and of the magnificent and astonishing triumph over a realm into which the princes of Rome never pushed their army. Having a confident hope in the fervour of your devotion, we believe it would be your desire, not only to conserve but *to extend the privileges of the Church of Rome*, and, as in duty bound, *to establish her jurisdiction where she has none at present;* we, therefore, earnestly exhort your Highness to preserve to us the privileges belonging to St. Peter in that land."

It began to appear that there were really two churches in Ireland. One was the Church of Rome, with its papal machinery, its Peter's pence, its strong arm to punish those who refused to adopt the new system, and its swarms of English monks as the managers of its affairs. They took everything into their hands—schools, monasteries, churches and parishes. The government was on their side. The invading king won the chieftains, and the chieftains placed the yoke on the clansmen. It was thenceforth a misfortune for one to have Irish blood in his veins; it was a crime to have a love for the truly ancient Church in his heart. "The real origin of Irish popery is the English invasion under Henry II." * Of this reign Hume says, "The Irish had been imperfectly converted to Christianity; and what the pope regarded as the surest mark of their imperfect conversion, they followed the doctrines of their first teachers, and had never acknowledged any subjection to the see of Rome." The chiefs became zealous papists. The parliament was Roman Catholic; the bishops were all appointed by the pope, and they had seats in the national councils; the kings were all "most dearly beloved sons of the pope, devout sons of the Church," whose will was law and power was supreme.

The other was the Church of Saint Patrick, greatly changed indeed, both in form and doctrine, but yet asserting her independence of Rome. It was a remnant saved from the general wreck. It endured severe persecution. "The Church of the native Irish was discountenanced and ignored by

* Soames, Lat. Church, p. 59.

Rome, as well as by England. It consisted of the old Irish clergy and inmates of the monasteries, who had not adopted the English manners or language, and who were therefore dealt with as rebels, and compelled to seek for support from the charity or devotion of the people. Many of these took refuge in foreign countries;" others still lingered in places where they waited for the dawn of a better day.* Then centuries later came the great Reformation. It revived the old spirit. Many received the gospel anew, and entered into the Reformed churches of England or of Scotland, and to our times there has been a force of staunch Protestants in Ireland, strongest in the northern counties, where Saint Patrick seems to have laid the most enduring foundations.

Strange reversals occur in history, and one of the strangest is, that the Irish people, who owed nothing to Rome for their conversion to Christianity, and who struggled long against her pretensions, should now be reckoned among her most submissive adherents. They once quoted Saint Patrick against her claims and customs, but now they associate their devotion to Patrick with their devotion to popery. Once he was their great protestant and

* Todd's St. Patrick, pp. 237-244.

the father of their Church; now they imagine that he was a papist, and they acknowledge the fatherhood of the man whose toe is kissed in the Vatican. Ireland hates England. Well she might, if the reason were that the English king Henry II. sold her fair domains to the pope and forced her to pay the Peter's pence. Before that time she might love England and hate Rome; now she has reversed her affection.

Beautiful Ireland, gem of the sea! Once the resort of students, the home of scholars, the abode of poetry, the nursery of orators, the light of Europe, the isle of saints! Along thy shores the voyager coasts, and he pities thee, now so oppressed by Rome, so darkened by the errors of a perverted religion, and he thinks what thou wouldst have continued to be had the Church of Saint Patrick never been overthrown!

Upon no other land did the darkness of the Middle Ages more slowly yet more thickly fall; over none did ministering angels longer hover to witness the courage of those who were the last to yield; in none was truth more completely crushed beneath the foreign invader's foot; from none was Christian liberty more thoroughly banished; and through none did superstition more boldly walk to banish God's holy word, turn history into legends, erase the early records of an independent Church, and overthrow the monuments of the ancient faith. In the course of centuries missionaries dwindled into monks, earnest pastors into exacting priests, ancient schools into monasteries; the pulpit with the Bible upon it fell back behind the altar set up for the mass and the waxen candle; the simple church was overshadowed by the cathedral; shrines were erected to saints, and devotion took the form of penance and pilgrimage. Ireland was laid at the feet of the so-called Virgin Mary, on whose brow was placed the crown that rightly belonged only to Christ. True, a small, hidden remnant remained, waiting for the Reformation. They accepted it when it came. Their sons nobly restored the ancient faith; their toil now is to bring Ireland back to the Church of Saint Patrick, so far as it was the body of Christ. In that restoration is the hope of Erin's deliverance. May Heaven speed the day!

CHAPTER XIII.

LAST DAYS.

WE have wandered. As the work was greater than the man, we have quite lost sight of him. He lived to see the Druids cast into the shade. They were no longer the power behind the throne. Some of them were converted; others grew sullen and silent. So many of the kings were at least nominally Christian that these men of the oaks dared not lift a hand against the missionaries. They might steal into the deep forests and cut the mistletoe, but their barbarous rites of sacrifice were ended.

The Druids had framed many of the old laws, and a reform was needed. The tradition is, that King Laogaire brought together a council of nine wise men to revise the laws of the realm and adapt them to the principles of the gospel. Three kings, three bishops and three bards are said to have sat together in the work:

> The bishops were the most devout Saint Patrick,
> The good Benignus and the wise Cairnech;

> The kings were Laogaire, the Irish monarch,
> A prince in heraldry exactly skilled;
> With him was joined the ever-prudent Daire,
> The warlike king of Ulster; and the third
> Was famous Corc, wide Munster's martial king,
> Whose love for letters proved his love for peace;
> The bards, well versed in the antiquities,
> Were faithful Dubtach and the sage Feargus,
> And Rosa, skilled in foreign languages:
> These nine conned o'er the annals and the laws,
> Erased the errors, the effects of fraud
> Or ignorance, and by the test of truth
> Made good the statutes and the histories.*

One of the works said to have come from the hands of this committee is the *Cain Patraic*, or "Patrick's Law." Perhaps it was begun in his time, but the greater part of it is ridiculous enough to have come only from the monks of a later age.†

To him a tract is often ascribed concerning the present world, heaven and hell. It is aptly entitled "The Three Habitations," in the first of which all the living now dwell, and in one of the other two every soul must abide after death. It makes no reference to purgatory. There is no proof that

---

* One ancient MS. bears the title of the Leabhar na Huaidh-chongabhala, a work into which we do not pretend to have dipped. It was highly approved by the three bards.

† Todd's St. Patrick, pp. 483, 484.

he wrote a word of it, nor has it any reference to the legend of "Saint Patrick's Purgatory," which has become proverbial. It seems that on a little island in Loch Erne a monastery grew up at a later day. When some of the inmates needed to be punished, they were sent to a cave near by to bring themselves into a better mood, or pilgrims were there placed to do penance for their sins. It was easy to imagine that through the gloomy cavern were seen the spirits of the unhappy, whose penance had not been sufficient upon earth. Wild tales were told about such visions in order to win more money from those who were made to believe that even Christians must be purified by suffering after death. To give force to the superstition the monks laid hold of the name of Patrick, which had a charm for the Irish ear and heart. It was declared that he had been in the cave, and there had a sight of the flames of purgatory.* An English knight named Owen went thither and shuddered at what he saw. An English monk wrote a pretended history of the place, and the gross imposture was supported for centuries by the Anglo-Irish bishops in Donegal in order to bring over the people to Rome. It is a specimen of the lying

* Camden, Britannia, p. 1019.

wonders fixed upon the popular Saint Patrick, and this is the foundation of his purgatory.

He believed that to the dying Christian the Lord was saying, "This day shalt thou be with me in Paradise." The true Church of St. Patrick held that man is naturally ignorant of the true God, and has nothing of his own but sin; that Christ is sufficient for the salvation of the sinner; that the sinner is saved by the grace of God, who brings him to a sense of his unbelief through faith in Christ, and not by his own works; that every saved sinner is constrained by love to be holy and do all the good he can, though he does not thereby gain any *merit;* and that when the believer dies he passes immediately into glory.*

Great was the love of the people for the zealous missionary, so well and so widely known. Thousands looked up to him as a father whose toils had been endured for their good. Not for himself, not for power, nor for his own glory, had he lived, but for them and for his Lord. They began to count the years when he must die. They looked upon his shorn head,† and thought of the crown of

* Wilson, Ch. of St. Patrick, p. 77.

† He was often called the *Tailcend,* "the shorn crown." It was a general custom of that age for the clergy to be marked

righteousness of which he was wont to speak. When they saw his gray hairs, they may have thought, as was said of another venerable man,

> When the snow on that mountain-top melts,
> There will be a great flood in this valley.

It appears that he worked on to the last. Only when his strength failed, he ceased to travel along the trodden paths, visit the churches already planted, plunge into new forests, enter among wild tribes, call for lodgings at the castles of warlike chiefs, expose himself to perils by robbers and murderers, search out the scattered sheep of his Master, found new churches, ordain new pastors and set them to feed the flock of God. But the time came when he could not ride so far by day, nor face the storm so bravely, nor so safely risk the cold, damp air of night. Not so early could he "rise up at the voice of the bird;" the silver cord was loosening, the golden bowl breaking, for he

by the tonsure. Perhaps it meant at first little more than the white cravat now does with some clergymen. But it became in the seventh century a weighty matter. Then it was found that the Irish tonsure was quite different from the Roman. In the Irish the head was shorn on the front, from one ear over to the other; in the Roman the whole top was made bare. The argument then was that the Irish clergy had Saint Patrick for their example. What grave disputes about trifles!

was going to his long home. Old age was creeping upon him. He had no earthly home, no family; no wife to sit by a hearthstone and talk of the past scenes on the way of their pilgrimage; no brothers in Ireland to invite him beneath a roof where he might take his last sleep, and on some morning be gone, to their surprise and grief; no sisters to make soft the last couch and press their warm hands upon his brow as it grew cold; and the only spot that he could claim as his own was the grave. Nor to that had he any title-deed; it must be granted in charity.

The story is, that a gentle voice whispered to him that he must soon rest from his labours. It was that of Brigid, whose name is linked with his in its vast popularity, and given to thousands of Irish children. The legend runs that she was "the daughter of a bard and a beautiful captive, whom her master had sent away, like Hagar, at the suggestion of his wife. Born in grief and shame, she was received and baptized along with her mother by the disciples of Saint Patrick. In vain would her father have taken her back and bestowed her in marriage when her beauty and wisdom became apparent. She devoted herself to God and the poor, and went to live in an oak wood, formerly consecrated to the false gods. . . . She founded the first female monastery which Ireland had known, under the name of Kildare, the cell of the oak." * It can hardly be denied that in the time of Patrick some pious women caught the spirit of a secluded life. Were it not for this, we should think that Brigid lived at a later age, if indeed she lived at all. Only a few grains of wheat can be winnowed from the bushels of chaffy legends which assume to be her history. Yet it is barely possible that, with tear-dewed hands, she embroidered a shroud for the body of Patrick when he should die.

The aged missionary could not forget the first spot of earth which he had secured for his Lord. The old barn, the Sabhal church, could not be deprived of his first love. About fifty years had passed since he had landed on its neighbouring shore. Thither he went to die in the arms of the brethren, who there had their home for study and the instruction of youth.† Their spiritual father of

* Montalembert, Monks of the West, ii. p. 393.

† It was another Patrick, who died at Glastonbury, in Wales. He seems to have been an abbot at Armagh, and to have died in 850 from the fury of the Danes. In later times he was confounded with his great namesake, and pilgrimages were made by the Irish to Glastonbury on account of Saint Patrick.

ninety-six years must have warned them against an abuse of devotion to study, and entreated them to go forth and preach to the ignorant tribes the name of Jesus. He was not a monk. He did not believe that monasteries were the chief places where the Lord dwelt. Perhaps he said as another advised in later times, " Go away from God, if you think he is only at a convent, and you will find him wherever you labour for him." Such, we think, would have been the counsel of Patrick.

When he died the sad report went forth afar, and in all the churches there was weeping. What a privilege to be at his funeral! The clergy gathered in large numbers to lay him in his grave. We give no credit to the legend that Armagh sharply disputed with Saul for his body, and that to settle the matter it was placed in a cart, and the oxen bidden to go whither they pleased, taking it to a place now called Downpatrick. When their father was to be buried the sons did not all become fools. They surely did not separate into armies, fighting for his remains, until the oxen decided the case, and then drop the feud. The simple fact seems to be that he was solemnly and honorably laid in a grave at Downpatrick, near the spot where he had first preached the gospel in Ireland.

The early Church of Saint Patrick seems not to have adored his relics. There was no virtue in his grave, that it should become a sacred place of resort. Those Christians kept no lights ever burning upon it. They reared no monument over it which time could not destroy. To it they made no pilgrimages, thus to win merit or to gain his favour as a patron saint. No shrine was there for the offerings of their penance. Had such been the case, his grave would certainly have been better known in after centuries. His name was written upon their hearts; his monument was the work that he had done for Christ. No other is so worthy of a good man, in whatever age he may live, or land he may toil.

The date of his death is fixed, by the Annals of Ulster, in the year 493,* nor is there any good reason to question it. That he was born, baptized and called from earth on a Wednesday is a mere tradition, framed to suit the Roman theories. The seventeenth of March is observed as "Saint Patrick's Day," but the day of his decease none can determine. It was a cunning artifice of Rome to seize upon the names of eminent Christians and claim them as her "saints." Even the apostles

---

* Thus also Ussher, Anc. Irish; Cave, Scrip. Eccl.

were taken by her craft, and their names enrolled upon her calendar, as if they had been one in faith with every Boniface and Gregory. Nor was this the worst. These "saints" came to be adored. The pope declared that they were worthy objects of general worship, and prayers were addressed to them as intercessors with God. Thus Patrick was captured by Roman hands, and set up as an idol for the people to adore. In one of the Irish Psalters he is mentioned as

> The divine Saint Patrick, who possessed
> The first place in the Irish calendar,
> And was the guardian angel of the isle.

And this saint-worship is not a folly of the past, when there was some excuse for ignorance. It is a sin of the present, and in our own land. It is approved by the highest authorities of the Roman Church in America. Those who offer "The Litany of Saint Patrick" repeat these words: "Saint Patrick, apostle of Ireland, model of bishops, profoundly humble, consumed with zeal, example of charity, glory of Ireland, instructor of little ones, our powerful protector, our compassionate advocate! pray for us!" The "Novena to Saint Patrick" is even worse; for in it are these petitions: "Glorious Saint Patrick! receive my prayers, and accept the sentiments of gratitude and veneration with which my heart is filled toward thee. . . . O charitable shepherd of the Irish flock! who wouldst have laid down a thousand lives to save one soul, take my soul and the souls of all Christians under thy especial care, and preserve us from the dreadful misfortunes of sin. . . . I most humbly recommend to thee this country [the United States], with that which was so dear to thee while on earth."*

To rescue the true Patrick from the hands of such Romanists, who insult God by adoring a good man, is a work that needs to be done. If the present attempt shall aid in such a result; if it be shown that they have no sort of claim to him; if the reader shall find evidence that he was a zealous missionary, who sought to win souls to Christ, and that, with all his errors, he was nevertheless one of the greatest men of his age, and if anything shall be found herein to kindle piety,—the effort may be blessed.

The God of Joseph was the God of Patrick. In the one case he permitted a Hebrew youth to be

* "The Golden Manual, being a Guide to Catholic devotion, &c. With the approbation of the Most Rev. John Hughes, Archbishop of New York." 1853.

taken from his home, and sold into Egypt for a great purpose; in the other, he had a wise design in so bringing good out of evil that a British lad was stolen from his parents and sold into Ireland. How dark was his providence to each of them in his younger days! How hard then to read his goodness in the event, and yet how plain his glory afterward! Each was a slave. "It is good for a man that he bear the yoke in his youth. He sitteth alone and keepeth silence, because he hath borne it upon him. He putteth his mouth in the dust: if so be there may be hope. He giveth his cheek to him that smiteth him; he is filled with reproach. For the Lord will not cast off for ever; but though he cause grief, yet will he have compassion according to the multitude of his mercies."* Each of these bondsmen in a foreign land was a dreamer of such dreams as God sent for good toward a people. Joseph is led to provide abundant stores of corn for a time of famine—Patrick is led to bear the bread of eternal life to a people famishing in sin. Each sees the mysteries of God open with mercies, and can thank him for the ways which were higher than his ways, and the thoughts which were above his thoughts. This

* Lamentations iii. 27-32.

parallel may have struck the mind of Patrick, and it is possible that he once used such words as are put into his mouth by one of his biographers: "I am here by the same Providence that sent Joseph into Egypt to save the lives of his father and brethren."

Still farther may we compare them. Joseph was faithful to his master, and thus won the favour of those who had the command of his services. Thus it seems to have been with young Patrick. Such a lesson should not be lost. Those who may be under the bidding of severe and exacting employers may gain their confidence by being faithful. This qualifies them for a good influence. Character speaks; the light shines; hardest hearts may be touched, and God may be glorified.

The Lord who heard young Patrick's prayer has never grown weary; never has he turned away his ear from the voice of the penitent, crying to him night and day, amid sunshine and in stormiest days; never was he slumbering when the seeker after God rose up to plead with him before the dawn. Thus Patrick sought the Lord amid the rains and snows and darkness; he found the ever-gracious Redeemer. Is any one now so earnest? Is any so devout? Patrick, God is waiting for the voice of prayer. The young exile found him a covenant-keeping God. To be born of Christian parents, to have been dedicated to the Lord in infancy, to be the child of prayers and tears, is a great privilege. Such a one has the noblest lineage. Let every one thus favoured think of the obligations that rest upon him. But grace is not inherited by birth—not even from a father who is a deacon, and a grandfather who is a presbyter. On that succession Patrick could not depend. He must remember his sins, repent, and accept the grace of the covenant made for his good, between his parents and their God, when he was baptized and consecrated to him. Who knows but that in virtue of the sign the Lord granted to him the things signified? Who knows but that for the sake of that covenant God remembered him in a strange land, turned the iron furnace into a school of prayer and piety, blessed him with the deliverance of his soul from sin, led him out of bondage and restored him to his father's house? Who knows but that his father and mother had often besought the Lord to make their son a preacher of the gospel, like his grandfather? Perhaps it was in answer to their prayers that Patrick became a missionary, so eminent in his day that he stands forth as the type of a class of Christian heroes, who plunged into deep forests and triumphed over the forces of barbarism.

What kindles the missionary spirit? What now will induce young men to make an effort for the salvation of the pagan world? Just what led Patrick to devote his life to the work—the love of God and the sad condition of the heathen. The one he had felt in his heart—the other he had seen with his eyes. Think of him tending the flocks on the hills, where he met not a man who knew of his God, his gospel, his heaven or his eternity. What a moral desert! Savage chiefs were ever plotting war, and degraded clansmen rushing to the fray. Barbarous revels were heard in the castles, and the howling of the Druids in the oaken forests. Robbers were the freemen; every child might be carried away and sold as a slave. He saw enough to sicken his heart. He pitied the heathen of Ireland, and no man will ever do his duty to the pagan world unless he is touched with a like compassion. You need not visit the heathen land; the picture of its woes may come in the next Christian magazine. An hour's study may waken the pity that will kindle the spirit to lend the needed aid. Patrick went himself. A world of work was before him. The mode of beginning it was simple; the courage to begin at all was sublime. But he pitied men, he prayed to God, he went everywhere preaching the Word, with love to sinners and an enthusiasm for Christ. There never was a harder field for labour. "There never was a nobler missionary than Patrick." There never was such a civilizing power as Christianity.

We surely may think of Patrick as a man who first entered Ireland as a slave, but who died in it a victor. Erin never knew his like. No other name was ever so stamped upon that island and her people. It is the very synonym of an Irishman; we expect him to answer to it. It is Ireland's compliment to her greatest Christian teacher. The Irish mother who gives it to her son bestows more real honour upon the memory of Saint Patrick than is rendered in all the prayers offered to him by the multitude of people who swear by his name and hold him as a guardian saint. We would restore his character, and remember him as a man who was fired with the missionary spirit; who braved the seas in his little boat and landed among strangers; who walked up from the shore to offer to the barbarians the greatest gift of heaven; who gathered about him a little circle of listeners, and moulded them into different men; who overthrew great idolatries, and raised the true cross of Jesus where had stood the altars of the Druids. His sphere enlarged. He stood before courts; he travelled through the counties. He dictated reforms to the monarch on the throne, and sought liberty for the menial beneath the thatch. He set on foot a system of schools, in which were reared kings for the crown, ministers for the State, Christian bards to make a nation's songs, and wise men to frame her laws, pastors for the gathering flocks and missionaries to foreign lands. In no small degree he changed the State and reared the Church. He put in motion the forces of a Christian civilization, no doubt taking up the measures which the Culdees had introduced before him, infusing a new spirit into their system, and bringing out of their secluded cells the light that was meant to shine forth into the broad world.

In such a man we ought to find much to imitate. Not faultless, not free from certain errors of his age, not a Paul of the first century, not a Judson of the nineteenth; yet he shared largely in the traits of an apostle and the devotion of a missionary. To preach Christ to the heathen was his great idea and purpose. With him the gospel was not simply a revelation of God's love to himself; not a gift which he could accept for himself alone, and retreat into some remote corner to study and cherish; it was a proclamation. It was something to be published, to be told everywhere, and to be urged upon the dullest ear and the hardest heart. He would be its herald, giving it forth to all men with a generous hand.

To live for Christ, as he thought, was not to be a monk; it was to be a missionary. This was his character. We doubt whether there was one other missionary in the fifth century who was his equal— one other so unresting, so ardent, so enthusiastic for souls, so stout in rough trials, and so anxious to lift up his voice in wilds where the name of Jesus had never been uttered. We doubt whether the example of any other man in that age did more to fire the hearts of young men with the missionary spirit. It was the burning coal in the Irish Church. When he was gone, an host of messengers arose, not to light a torch at the king's flame, and run over the hills with "the fiery cross" of the Druids, but to touch Patrick's burning coal with their lips, and hasten afar with the name of Christ to the perishing. Despite the tendency in Irishmen to become monks, no other land in that age sent forth more missionaries. Ireland then excelled Rome in the work of publishing the gospel. Hear one of them of the ninth century, Claude Clement, who is said to have founded the University of Paris under Charlemagne, and then gone into Northern Italy. He says: "When I came to Turin, I found all the churches full of abominations and images; and because I began to destroy what every one adored, every one began to open his mouth against me. They say, 'We do not believe there is anything divine in the image; we only reverence it in honour of the individual whom it represents.' I answer, If they who have quitted the worship of devils, honour the images of saints, they have not forsaken idols—they have only changed their names; for whether you paint upon a wall the pictures of St. Peter or St. Paul, or those of Jupiter or Mercury, they are now neither gods, nor apostles, nor men. The name is changed: the error continues the same. . . . If the cross of Christ ought to be adored because he was nailed to it, for the same reason we ought to adore mangers, because he was laid in one; and swaddling-clothes, because he was wrapped in them. We are not ordered to adore the cross, but to bear it, and deny ourselves. Shall we not believe God when he swears that neither Noah, nor Daniel, nor Job shall deliver son or daughter by their righteousness; for this end he makes the declaration, that none might put confidence in the intercession of the saints."* This learned and zealous man may have imitated Saint Patrick, but he did not worship him. He swept out of the churches of Piedmont the Roman novelties, and aided the ancient Waldenses in bringing the people back to the old religion of apostolic days.

A late Roman Catholic author, ashamed of the puerilities of Joceline, and yet anxious to set forth Patrick as the "patron Saint of the Emerald Isle," if not of all America, says of him, in about the best passage of his book: " He found it a task much more arduous to reform the heart and root out paganism and vice, when fortified by custom and long habits; but his constant application to the great work, his patience, his humility and invincible courage, conquered all opposition. Divine Providence .... endued this champion of the gospel with all the natural qualities which were requisite for the functions of an apostle. His genius was sublime and capable of the greatest designs; his heart fearless; his charity was not confined to

* Usher, Religion Anc. Irish.

words and thoughts, but shone out in works and actions, and extended itself to the service of his neighbours, to whom he carried the light of the gospel."*

We close in harmony with the final sentence of the Confession: "I pray those who believe and fear God, and who may condescend to look into this writing, which Patrick the sinner, an unlearned man, wrote in Hibernia, if I have done or established any little thing according to God's will, that not a man of them will ever say that my ignorance did it; but think ye and let it be verily believed that it was the gift of God."

* Life of St. Patrick, published by Murphy, 1861.

THE END.

www.ingramcontent.com/pod-product-compliance
Lightning Source LLC
Chambersburg PA
CBHW021938240426
43669CB00047B/512